QUESTIONS & ANSWERS

PUBLISHED [IN THE NET] FOR INDIAN POLITICIANS:

By Hari Pada Roychoudhury

Copyright © Hari Pada Roychoudhury 2024
All Rights Reserved.

ISBN 979-8-89446-333-9

DEDICATION

The book is dedicated to my beloved country men who are involved as political workers to give their service for the well being of the people and the prosperity of the country instead of the prosperity of the self image and the future prosperity of his or her own family. Although GANDHI being the FATHER of the Nation in spite of the KILLING of thousands of Hindu Bengalis and Punjabis and displaced them as Refugees by the division of INDIA and compelled them to left their ancestral homes for the safety of their lives.

Contents

PREFACE

 , 

No-1 No-2 No-3

No 1. Who Divided India just to kick out Jinnah.

No 2. Who Sacrificed Tibet to China out of fear

No 3. Who foolishly Divided Bengal by the cry of Hindu Home Land and foolishly sacrificed life in the JAIL of Kashmir.

(3 Destroyers of INDIA):

For the cause of Independence at the very outset the name of Bhagat Singh will come in front, a Sikh who belongs to a Punjabi family of great leaders. He was so brave and didn't fear for anything; the fighter fought so hard and sacrificed his life for the freedom and independence of our country. Then comes Bal Gangadhar Tilak, a famous freedom fighter of India. He was born in 1856. He plays a very important role in freedom and independence of India and sacrifices a lot for freedom. He motivated Indian people to make unity and fight for independence and their rights.

Then the name of Subhas Chandra Bose, known by the nick name Netaji. He was a brave and strong leader that forced the Britishers to leave India. Subhas established the Indian National Army and made a very popular slogan "Give me blood, and I shall give you freedom".

But there are many so-called freedom fighters such as Gandhi, Nehru and others. Here in the book their activity is highlighted through question and answers.

It should not be forgotten that India is a God gifted land nowhere present in the world but few so called freedom fighters instead of bringing prosperity to the nation destroyed the nation INDIA for their personal name and fame. Why it is God gifted, because it has agricultural Land, rivers for plenty of useful water, and Hills and Minerals everywhere but the country was subjected to a beggar's country by the activity of few Indian Politicians.

The Religion Islam came following the death of Muhammad in 632 CE and expanded over a vast geographical area; conversion to Islam was boosted by Arab Muslim forces expanding over vast territories and building imperial structures over time although the Arab Land in desert Area including its nearby area Iraq, Jordan, Qatar and Abu Dhabi emirate. Now the whole region is a glorious place of prosperity by the discovery of Oil.

In the beginning for their survival they came to India and India was ruled by the Sultans and then by the Mughals bringing development and prosperity in India.

England was a small region, they got United by their small Islands, forming the UK and came to India for business to survive. Finally they Ruled India establishing British Rule in India and achieved freedom finally but Indian leaders destroyed beautiful India by their selfish character to make name and fame for themselves. Now forgetting the period of "NON VIOLENCE" India is in the path of the RULE OF RIGHT under Modi Government hoping for a better INDIA getting free from BEGGAR's INDIA under "NON-VIOLENCE" of Gandhi.

Islam is the majority religion in several subregions: Central Asia, Western Asia, North Africa, West Africa, the Sahel, and the Middle East. The diverse Asia-Pacific region contains the highest number of Muslims in the world, surpassing the combined Middle East and North Africa.

After the United States achieved its independence from Britain, America expanded westward through military conquest and the purchase of colonial territories. Saudi Arabia, a land of desert and the USA, a land of cold all developed leading a life of prosperity to its citizens while India, a land of Natural wealth was converted to a beggar's place by the selfish Indian politicians.

Questions & Answers

Q.No. 1 - Most recently Published Why do Muslims of Kashmir in the Part of Pakistan want to join INDIA?

Muslims of Pakistan were once Indian brothers. (Once during the period of Akbor attempts have been made to create one religion.) Creation of Pakistan was a blunder by Jinnah and Gandhi. Now time has come to reunite the two countries. Religion cannot separate the two brothers. Few days ago **they were Hindus. Change of religion is nothing but a belief which is** unknown. Think of Russia and the Lincoln Period of the USA. No religion, today they are superpowers. Had it been a UNITED British INDIA, it would be a superpower. An intelligent person sometimes makes compromises even with an enemy for the cause of public benefit.

Unity is the source of development. Division of India is the cause of destruction and it was due to the rivalry of Gandhi & Jinnah. After all the people of India -Pakistan were the brothers & Sisters. Islam has come from Arab countries but the religion is not everything rather economic progress is everything.

It is necessary to get back to British India for the progress and prosperity of the region forgetting Gandhi and religion. If the British and French could live together why not India, Pakistan and Bangladesh live together for the betterment and progress of the region and the people.

Q.No. 2 - Why do POK people want to merge in India? Is this the Modi effect of politics?

Indian Kashmir under the Modi Government has changed remarkably. Indian new Kashmir has seen new road networks, bridges and the construction of one of Asia's largest tunnels in recent years. In 1947, Pakistan took the shortcut to economic development; Mohammad Ali Jinnah had been assured by Winston Churchill and later governments that Pakistan would be developed via investments from abroad. Mr. Jinnah would perish waiting (while in a broken ambulance) in Karachi just a year into Pakistan's beginnings into misadventures, military coups, and status as a near failed state. Mohammad Ali Jinnah knew full well in 1946 that Pakistan would go on a very different course of development, as Western military bases would be not only allowed in Pakistan but would have to be encouraged in order to ensure assistance would flow into Pakistan. Initially, Pakistan would develop at a far more rapid pace with modern airports, highway systems and GDP growth. The Pakistan Army invasion of the Kingdom of Kashmir had been done during Jinnah's brief period of leadership; the British though in charge of Pakistan's army had clandestinely allowed the invasion. The nexus of Pakistan joining the West in what would become a standard of Cold War Policy was occurring. India would be denied a border with Afghanistan and a pathway to energy exports from the Soviet Union. Pakistan would be responsible for combating Soviet influence in Afghanistan; a second act of the Great Game had begun. Nearly one third of Kashmir would be occupied by Pakistan, while India would retain slightly more than half after China both invaded Aksai Chin and was given disputed territory by Pakistan in 1962 and 1963 respectively. Pakistan set a modern precedence by gifting disputed territory to China which accepted it as a border settlement in 1963. The reality was Pakistan sought Chinese Atomic assistance which the U.S. would acquiesce to as part of Cold War Policies. Three full scale wars would be initiated by Pakistan against India; ultimately Pakistan would lose control of East Pakistan following genocide of three million Hindus and Sikhs by the Pakistan Army. The genocide would end with an Indian victory in the third Indo-Pakistan war in 1971. Pakistan would lose both its status as the most populous Muslim nation as well as any semblance of parity it had with India was gone. Pakistan's economic growth slowed during the 1970s as the effects of the war with India created economic disruption and a loss of half of Pakistan's tax base. U.S. pressure to destabilize Afghanistan in the 1970s had created another destination for Pakistan's capital. Pakistani Occupied Kashmir was hardly even thought about in economic terms as it was a rallying cause for the Pakistan Military to use against India. Pakistan's diversion of the radicals it had trained alongside the U.S. during their war on the Soviet Union in Afghanistan during the 1980s would cause both an insurgency in Indian Punjab and later in Indian Kashmir. Yet this all would fail to stop India's economic growth after 1992. Pakistan's economic decline is a serious threat to regional stability. The divergence of India's economic growth from the lessening interest of the West in Pakistan after the end of Cold War, seemingly caught Pakistan off guard and it had never planned for an event where foreign aid would begin lessening. Pakistan would get a reprieve from this during the Musharaf era as the U.S. once more capitalized Pakistan's economy to ensure Pakistan waged Bush's vision of the War on Terror, though it seems Pakistan's military establishment once more used the funds more to ensure its own survival. Osama Bin Laden would be found right under the thumb of Pakistan's military establishment in Abbott bad in 2011. The U.S. reaction though was not to place sanctions or any real punitive measures. Geopolitically, it tells a lot about the relationship and war on terror which had been diverted to Iraq under the false pretexts of weapons of mass destruction. Pakistan occupied Kashmir would by the second decade of this century begin to see its development status gap with Indian Kashmir become larger by the year. Prime Minister Modi would fully integrate Kashmir into the Indian Union undoing years of Congress policies of treating Kashmir as a separate region under Indian administration. The differences in Kashmir's economy were near immediate. Today, Indian Kashmir has soaring real-estate prices, billions in infrastructure investments, and long-term development projects. Pakistan occupied Kashmir is part of a nation which had to once more be bailed out by the U.S. controlled International Monetary Fund. Pakistan also would see its own elected Prime Minister; Imran Khan be removed by a "sudden" vote in Pakistan's parliament as Imran Khan began to discuss openly about the ruination of Pakistan by its outside handlers. Pakistan's population was jolted into realizing just where their nation had begun and where it had arrived. Protest in Pakistan Occupied Kashmir against economic woes and hard-line treatment by the Pakistani Army. The differences in development are increasing with each passing year. Pakistan Occupied Kashmir perhaps more than other regions have far less vested in propagating the message Pakistan's military has dictated. Pakistani Kashmir neither feels it is fully integrated, nor has it seen economic progress in decades. POK supplies much of Pakistan's power grid with electricity but residents of POK pay higher electric prices. Once more Pakistan is facing accusations that its portion of Punjab is preferred over all other regions in Pakistan. Pakistan Occupied Kashmir even has had protests where many on the border with India asked Prime Minister Modi to free them from illegal occupation. The real message here is that suffering in Pakistan is becoming harder for many, but regions which are essentially occupied are becoming vocal. As the economic gap between India increases, many in Pakistan are questioning the two-nation theory, as it neither brought prosperity to Pakistan nor changed the standing of Indian Muslims in the world. Jinnah and the British Empire had proclaimed Pakistan as the "Homeland of Indian Muslims", Pakistan never became this place. Pakistan Occupied Kashmir is realizing its plight in deeper ways as the decades have passed.

What about Bengal and Bengali Language?

Bengalis language is not expanded but instead destroyed by Bengali Hindus who were foolish and emotional with the belief of many Hindu Gods adverse to Russia of Stalin. Raja Ram Mohan Roy was the only intelligent far-sighted Bengali who said that the Bengali got the power of administration due to the sacrifice of the British who defeated the Muslim Ruler Sirajudulla and handed over the administration to the Bengali Hindus. If they were intelligent, they could expand the Bengali language to Bonga-Bihar-Urrisia and then to the whole of India and the World. But instead, they danced with Gandhi and spoiled the backbone of Bengalis by destroying all the industries of Bengal which are now in Gujarat, and finally by the division of Bengal and Bengali Language under the Leadership of short-sided Bengal Leader Dr. Shyama Prasad Mukherjee who died in Kashmir Jail destroying Bengal and Bengali Language. (Mr. Mukherjee never visited the rural Bengal, so he thought of Hindu Home Land keeping in mind the Brahamins of CALCUTTA.)

Q.No. 3 - Why do POK people want to merge in India? Is this the Modi effect of politics?

It is nothing but foolishness not to talk with Pakistan. Who were Pakistanis? They were our brothers and sisters.

All were born and brought up in India (under the same custom). It is only a belief of Islam that has originated in Arab Land that has been spread here. But how can a brother be a no-brother? It was only Gandhi, a selfish cowardly person who brought the difference between Hindus and Muslims of Indians through the ethics of "NON-VIOLENCE" for his own image by removing efficient Jinnah and bringing foolish Nehru into the Chair.

Bengal was a place of humanity but it turned Islam for power politics.

Q.No. 4 - Would India be a better country had Pakistan and Bangladesh still been a part of it?

Yes, (definitely). Why should Bangladesh be divided into Hindu Bangobhumi and Buddha Bhumi? All human beings are the creatures of God if so all are equal. Unity is strength. We must learn how to live together and how to win the hearts of everyone. If India remained united the country would have been a Super-power. Those who divided British India are the destroyer of India. So Gandhi or Jinnah is the destroyer of British India. Pakistan or the recent Bangladesh is made up of the people of India. Today India is living with different names but the people's heart remains the same. Their joy of happiness brings happiness to every heart and again the sorrow of suffering brings the pain of sorrow to every heart of Indians. Why not we all get together to form the UNITED INDIA once again forgetting Gandhi?

Why didn't the Bengali Language develop?

Bengalis language is not expanded but instead destroyed by Bengali Hindus who were foolish and emotional with the belief of many Hindu Gods adverse to Russia of Stalin. Raja Ram Mohan Roy was the only intelligent far-sighted Bengali who said that the Bengali got the power of administration due to the sacrifice of the British who defeated the Muslim Ruler Sirajudulla and handed over the administration to the Bengali Hindus. If they were intelligent, they could expand the Bengali language to Bonga-Bihar-Urrisia and then to the whole of India and the World. But instead, they danced with Gandhi and spoiled the backbone of Bengalis by destroying all the industries of Bengal which are now in Gujarat, and finally by the division of Bengal and Bengali Language under the Leadership of short-sided Bengal Leader Dr. Shyama Prasad Mukherjee who died in Kashmir Jail destroying Bengal and Bengali Language.

Q.No. 5 - Why was India so poor after independence?

It was because of a few Indian selfish leaders who wanted only self-image, name, and fame and nothing else. Who is the destroyer of India No1 Gandhi, No2 Dr. B R Amedkar **(and)** No.3 Nehru

Jinnah created Pakistan only with 20% Muslims, he created Calcutta Killing, a hero while Gandhi hiding, a coward. Gandhi could not do anything with 80% of Hindus. B R Ambedkar threatened another Dalit State, he was satisfied with F (Constitution). Is he thought for all? Never, a Narrow-minded leader who never thought for all people. All destroyer's names must be removed for a better FUTURE INDIA.

Q.No. 6 - Would India be a better country had Pakistan and Bangladesh still been a part of it?

Yes (definitely). Why should Bangladesh be divided into Hindu Bango-bhumi and Buddha-Bhumi? All human beings are the creatures of God if so all are equal. Unity is strength. We must learn how to live together and how to win the hearts of everyone. If India remained united the country would have been a Super-power. Those who divided British- India are the destroyer of India. So Gandhi or Jinnah is the destroyer of British-India. Pakistan or the recent Bangladesh is made up of the people of India. Today India is living with different names but the people's heart remains the same. Their joy of happiness brings happiness to every heart and again the sorrow of suffering brings the pain of sorrow to every heart of Indians. Why not we all get together to form the UNITED INDIA once again forgetting Gandhi?

Q.No. 7 - What are the dark secrets of Mahatma Gandhi that are not taught in schools? (or in any other learning center)?

Dark Secrets:

1. To kick out Jinnah because Jinnah made a name in Bombay Court by the release of popular leader Tilak while Gandhi was afraid of facing the Judge on behalf of his first client in life.

2. To make a name and fame he required Nehru as the PM of India because he was not a fit person to be the PM. So he required Nehru, son of a Rich Person to enter and Jinnah, a Muslim out.

3. His movement of "Non-Violence" was only for his image only with the Hindus. Muslims making and training Muslim youths for Calcutta Rioting was good for him as it would help to divide India when

Jinnah will be out of India when he will be free to make Nehru the PM. So he was silent during the training of MUSLIM Youths for rioting.

4. He likes to live for his name and fame only, so he saved himself by hiding on the Calcutta Killing Day, 16ᵗʰ August 1946. He also saved his life on the 16ᵗʰ of August, the first Flag hoisting Ceremony of India's Independence by fledging away from Delhi to Calcutta for the safety of his life where the militant Punjabi Refugees in Delhi threatening all the Congress leaders - what kind of Independence it is by making the Hindu, Sikh Punjabis Refugees- who can kill each and every leaders.

5. He agrees secretly to the division of India because Jinnah was powerful with the militant Muslim League, who can bring once again the Mughal Dynasty back to India. So he avoided the Muslim popular Leader SIMANTA Gandhi, Khan Abdur Gaffer Khan who was dead against the division of India.

Q.No. 8 - An analysis of INDIA and other Nations:

India is a country full of natural resources but still a country of beggars compared to other developed countries - Other countries such as the USA, UK, European Countries including French, German etc- why? The USA, UK, French and other European countries are the regions of cold weather, the regions of the Arab countries are the desert regions but not India- but why did India remain undeveloped- why? The reason is simple. Most of the Indian political leaders were selfish, self centered and narrow minded. In short, I am an Author taking the names of a few Indian leaders, Gandhi in particular, who discarded the real Indian HERO Subas Bose (Netaji). He made the Indians a fool for his self image making Jinnah, a talented advocate and politicians an enemy because of his inferiority and discarded him by the policy of religion of "NON-VIOLENCE" dividing India and destroying India but increasing himself to the position of FATHER of the nation and internationally a MAN OF PEACE killing millions by rioting and displacing millions of Bengalis and Punjabis from their ancestral Homes.

But in other countries we could see Lincoln as President of the USA united the blacks and whites and hence the development of the nation and not for himself, Similarly Willston Cherchill as the PM of UK during war time saved the nation from the attack of Hitler and did not surrender like Gandhi. The UK and French remained together during the two world wars even though they fought each other for more than 100 years, which is totally absent among the nations of India and its neighbours although they were alike in speaking, nature and culture only due to the selfish character of few India politicians.

Jinnha successfully created Pakistan due to the acceptance Partition formula by Petal who once thought to be the future PM of India, similarly Shyama Prasad Mukherjee thought to be the hero by the slow-gone of HINDU HOME LEAD instead of Sovereign UNITED BENGAL which was supported by the brother of Netaji along with Suwardy the then PM of Bengal who corrected his mistake of carrying out the CALCUTTA Killing. But S P Mukherjee instead of creating HINDU Home Land was compelled to leave the Ministry, compelled to go Kashmir and died in Jail custody. Is it his patriotic activity to save the Bengalis or destroying the Bengalis?

Rabridra & Nazrul are the souls of Bengalis, their soul lives in United Bengal.

Q.No. 9 - Was there a hurry for the British to leave India?

There was no hurry for the British to leave India so long Gandhi was busy with "Non-Violence". It is understood by the British that Gandhi wanted the British to stay in India for a longer time to increase his popularity and image but the British was in hurry to leave India after the War because Azad Hindu Force was the Indian Force under Netaji, in India every people, every Indian soldiers were sympathetic to the Azad Hind Force. So the British thought it wise to leave India as soon as possible for the safety of the British.

Q.No. 10 - What was Mahatma Gandhi's opinion of the Indian National Congress?

Mahatma Gandhi had no far sighted vision. His only vision was how to make a name and fame for himself. Otherwise, the condition of India would not be so pathetic and the people would not pass a beggars' life. He was responsible for Hindu-Muslim rivalry, rioting and what not. Today India would be a super-power. But Gandhi had destroyed India. British India is the India built by the Indian people and served each other with love, friendship and brotherhood. India will be again a powerful country if we could get back British India although divided but still we could improve relations and still we could restore the brotherhood as existed in between England and French.

Q.No. 11 - Do you think Narendra Modi secretly hates Mahatma Gandhi and wants to replace Gandhi's legacy with his own?

There is a saying that legacies are meant to be rewritten by hard work and by dedication. No doubt Modi is dedicated to the idea of India, but saying that he hates Mahatma Gandhi and wants to replace his legacy is wrong.

These words took buzz in the political arena after the current Gandhi, Sonia Gandhi who thinks herself and her political heirs Rahul Gandhi, Priyanka Gandhi to be the real Gandhi today said Gandhiji was feeling sad after 2014.

Even Gandhi had said in his last time after though split into two, India having attained political independence through means devised by the Indian National Congress, the Congress in its present shape and form, i.e., as a propaganda vehicle and parliamentary machine, has outlived its use.

So I don't think Modi is trying to replace Gandhiji, but he is surely trying to replace the idea born in politics by Sonia Gandhi, who was leading to a dead end of Indian politics with serious threat to the Nation idea of being one.

Now the question is more in terms of Congress where Sonia had said BJP is trying to replace the idea of Gandhiji with RSS ideology. They are a threat to democracy.

With the second term of BJP running under Modi, I till today didn't find any threat to democracy. If Congress is out of power and the government running corruption free is a threat to democracy is what Sonia Meant means, then I am ready to give more coming years to Modi.

If CBI, ED opening the account of corrupt politicians is a threat to Democracy then I am also fine with that Democracy.

Gandhiji was a big advocate of Make in India, Swachh Bharat Mission. I find Modi being more serious of thinking of Gandhiji than Sonia or Rahul.

Today the world has marched ahead, wherein every country in the world is trying to make it strong diplomatically as well as economically.

So if you think somebody would slap you and you show another cheek then they will leave you then you are wrong.

In Kashmir till today Pakistan was using the minds of local Kashmiri to exploit against India, What earlier Congress was doing they were waiting for Pakistan to change, but did you find it working. I think Never rather the same Pakistan terrorist invoked more terrorism in India and did more major blasts.

It would be wrong if we try to understand the policy of Ganhdiji to people like Hafeez Saeed.

Friendship with Snakes is always dangerous whereas UPA policies were helping the Snake to leave its poison in India.

So the time has gone to provide another cheek, but what Modi did was the right way and justified, today Pakistan is asking help across the whole world having been slapped tightly diplomatically in every front on both sides of the face.

Now coming back to democracy, Modi is our Prime Minister. He is elected by the will of Indians by a proper democratic process, It's not that he became PM by himself.

So if Gandhiji was a follower of non violence and peace, he believed in Democracy then Congress and Sonia should also accept the truth that they have been defeated twice by the democratic Process and they should also follow the same and try reviving them.

Let us remember what was said once by Jinnah, Jinnah said, in the dying bed, the greatest blunder, he did by dividing India.

So now India and Pakistan are able to settle all their differences amicably, who will be the biggest loser and who will be the biggest winner in such a scenario, no one but the Indian people.

It was Gandhi who was the destroyer of India by confirming the division of India as Hindu, Muslim. Once all were Indians, All were human beings of Indian soil with the same food, custom and nature. They will be happy only when they live, forgetting all kinds of rivalry. Unity is the source of progress and prosperity.

Rabridra & Nazrul are the souls of Bengalis, their soul lives in United Bengal.

Why was Winston Churchill so popular with the British people, and why is he still considered one of the greatest leaders in history?

He saved the UK from the worrier Hitler by his forceful voice of war.

Q.No. 12 - Why were there differences between Mahatma Gandhi and Bhimrao Ambedkar?

Both were self centered and selfish people. Gandhi tried to increase his image by making Nehru the PM of India while Ambedkar tried to increase his image by keeping reservations for his own community. Both were working against the UNITY and PROSPERITY of India. So, both were the real destroyer of INDIA in the formation of a UNITED India.

Q.No. 13 - Why did Mahatma Gandhi launch the non-cooperation movement? Also, why was it withdrawn?

Gandhi started the non-cooperation movement to increase his image. After returning from London with the paper degree of Barrette-Law, he started the practice at Bombay but failed miserably and realized law practice was impossible for him. Getting an opportunity to save the face he went to South Africa but returned to India in 1915. By the time Jinnah started the law practice at Bombay after Barrette- Law degree from Inner Temple London like Gandhi. At the very beginning he was successful in releasing the most favorite Leader BAL Gangadhar Tilak from jail. As such his popularity increased tremendously and he became an Ambassador of Hindu-Muslim Unity. Gandhi was unhappy with it. He thought of starting a non-cooperation movement through "Non-Violence" relating to "Ahingsa" connected with Hindu religion to downgrade Jinnah. He was thinking about how to increase his image by "Non-Violence". He satisfied the Hindus exposing himself as a SAINT with a half-naked dress of FAKIR as well as satisfied the British because the movement was free from violence. Of course to increase his popularity he supported the first world War at the beginning and at the end supported the Khilafat Movement to increase his popularity among the Muslims. He was indifferent to rioting or killing of village people due to Non-Violence because his only objective was to increase his image by kicking out Jinnah by division of the country and making Nehru the PM of India. After getting the right atmosphere he withdrew the "Non-Violence" movement and started the movement "Karo or Moro" to get independence and to make himself the FATHER of the nation by making Nehru the PM of India.

In order to know LONDON and the activity of Gandhi in London, the Author once thought to go to England, however he engaged himself to know the mystery of science, and finally he become a research worker to UMIST of UK, and became a professor of UMIST, and finally returned to India to serve the nation. At last the Author became an advocate to study the laws of the land, to know the reason for the poor conditions of the people in comparison to western life.

According to me as an Advocate, most of the politicians were busy with how to capture power and money by exploiting the common people for the betterment of the nation. If there be anybody at the top, who is no other than the Great Gandhi, who had no other skill except the orthodox religion, although he had a law degree from Inner Temple, although he tried to practice law at Bombay, but was a complete failure, rescued by Motilal Nehru, who never hesitated to divide the country as he was a coward politician, no parallel with Jinnah, removed Jinnah with secret understanding by dividing the county bringing Nehru in front, who had been made a politician, who had no political IQ except the sexy life with Mountbatten and many other Girls, like the so called Saint Gandhi, what is known to everyone, how he could bath with beautiful girl, how he could sleep naked with two girls in spite of objection from his close associates in Sabarmati Ashram. The secret pact, made a foolish, sexy, luxurious wealthy son (by dint of Father's property, contributing zero, unlike Jinnah & Jinnah house) Nehru the PM to make himself the FATHER of the nation and by Nehru's patronage he became an International ICON of peace subsiding the killing of millions Punjabis and Bengalis and displacing the millions. If Gandhi is called the greatest enemy of humanity, it would be less.

Killing people is BARBARISM, and everywhere it is done with heroism, Abraham Lincoln killed millions of people with heroic Barbarism for which USA today is a super power, Barbarism continued in French, for which democracy was established in France after French Revolution. Gandhi carried out cowardice, the worst kind of wicked Barbarism in the name of "non-Violence" taking the advantage of Hindu Bengali's religious weakness and foolishness to destroy the common people particularly in Bengali of Bengal subjecting them to kill in famine after famine just to make name and fame for himself acting as a secret agent of British. The aim was to capture power somehow, let the country go to hell. It is now even after 70 years that we could see Hindu-Muslim Mujaffarabad's worst killing of rioting where little children were killed. Is it Gandhi's rightful honor to be a man of peace, rather a man of killer for name and fame ever born in the UNIVERSE? Now my last wish is to see a corruption free

India under Modi, and a country of one nation with one Indian identity before my death.

Gandhi was the destroyer of India by division of India on the basis of religion and B.R. Ambedkar, an educated short sighted **Dalit** lawyer, was the destroyer of India by dividing the Indians on the basis of castes outlined in the constitution for reservation instead of reservation for economically backward sections of the society. All these leaders were short sighted and worked for self interest. Gandhi having being a Inner Temple Barrister brought religion in a clever way designing himself a saint with a half naked Fakir Dress just to be-fool the common Hindu religious minded people to accomplish his secret mission of bringing Nehru in the chair of PM and placing himself in the post of icon without caring the common Indians.

Today even after 70 years Indians are facing Hindu-Muslim rioting because of Gandhi and now people are fighting among themselves with Dalit-NonDalit because of the short sighted leader like B.R.Ambedkar.

Q.No. 14 - What about Nathuram Godse & Gandhi?

Nathuram Godse is definitely greater than Gandhi because of the mere selflessness of intention. Gandhi was not a person who would have sacrificed his own popularity for the country, however Godse was ready to sacrifice his own popularity, goodwill and respect in society for the country.

The problem is that Congress did not teach people about Godse as they taught people about their own poster boy Gandhi. As Congress was a British founded, British funded party they always took great care in promoting their own beliefs, leaders and criticizing the opposition's leaders and beliefs. This continued before and after Independence both. Punishments for Congressmen were lenient and for no Congressmen was harsh as it was a British patronized party. They created a perception for decades that there was nothing above the Congress and gullible people fell for it.They wrote gloriously about their own leaders and either sidelined or criticized leaders of the opposition.

Let us uncover some history on Godse for a change. Congress shared so little about Godse that most people think he was a hit man, but that wasn't so. He was a well educated, well respected Editor in Chief of the magazine Agrani. In the era when the Nizam's razakars spread mayhem and openly carried out murders and rapes, Godse as a part of an RSS delegation went to Hyderabad in 1939. He was arrested by the Nizam and sentenced to imprisonment including 250 whiplashes in which the whip was of a kind which would embed deep into the skin after coming in contact with it and had to be pulled out with effort before the next lash could be given. Godse bore this gory punishment. He spent months in Nizam's imprisonment in which he was whipped and starved without food or water for days.

Godse blamed Gandhi's flip flop stand on partition and was convinced that had Gandhi stood firm then the partition would never have happened. Godse decided to shoot Gandhi taking these facts in consideration: a) Gandhi made a weak stand on partition b) Gandhi openly criticized Hindus leaving Pak and coming to India after the partition though these poor people had no other country to go. Whereas Gandhi encouraged Indian Muslims wanting to go to Pak on their own will to remain in India and not go elsewhere c) when Gandhi was in Delhi after the partition he was brought the news of Hindu refugees from Pak taking shelter in a Delhi mosque, and he stone heartedly sent them a message that mosques are for Muslims and in heavy rains on that day these people had no other choice but to come on the streets. Whereas Gandhi made no such statement on Muslim refugees transiting to Pak who took refuge in Temples d) Gandhi went on a satyagraha to ensure that

Pak receives Rs 55 crore funding (big amount in that era) from India even when he knew that this money would be used against India e) Gandhi had the habit of teaching Ahimsa to the victim and never to the oppressor whereas the exact opposite holds sense. Gandhi even condemned greats like Maharana Pratap or Chhatrapati Shivaji Maharaj on Guru Govind Singh who taught us the values of self defence.

Given above points it was clear that Gandhi had lost his marbles but there was no one who could control the insanity Gandhi was upto as due to his flip flops more people died in partition violence than the number of people who died in Hitler's concentration camps or the holocaust. Though Godse became a hated figure he saved the souls of Hindus in India. But ironically the same Hindus whom he tried to save from being victimized today debate on whether Godse was greater or Gandhi was.

After Godse was hanged the Congress tried hard to impose bans on sharing details on the speech made in court by Godse, however today Godse's viewpoints can be read in his book 'Why I Killed Gandhi' or can be watched in a recent film of the same name on Limelight OTT website.

QNo.15 - What is the difference between Mahatma Gandhi and Netaji Subhash Chandra Bose? Why are they both respected by Indians of all ages?

Gandhi was a clever person who satisfied the Hindus by the Hindu movement of "Ahingsa or Non-Violence" and so the Hindus consider him a great SAINT because of his half naked Dress but they realised later how he cheated them by the division of the country making his favourite Nehru the PM and kicking out Jinnah to Pakistan to make himself world famous while Netaji gave his life fighting against the British forming "Azad Hind Fouz" for an Independent United India. Thus Gandhi was with "NON-VIOLENCE" while Netaji was with "VIOLENCE".

Q.No16 - What are Mohandas Gandhi's sons doing now?

Mahatma Gandhi had four sons, Harilal, Manilal, Devdas and Ramdas. All of them took part in the Indian independence movement, and none of them are alive now. The first and the most controversial among Gandhi's children, Harilal died within months of Gandhi's assassination. Ramdas, the last son died in 1969, the centenary year of the Mahatma. Among the third generation Gandhis, Gopalkrishna

Gandhi and Rajmohan Gandhi are more well known, while others are not much known in the public sphere.

Ironically none of them, except perhaps Gopal krishna Gandhi, involved themselves seriously in post independent Indian politics, despite being the progeny of the man considered the chief architect of the country's freedom movement and revered as "The Father of the Nation" and even their legitimate surname has been hijacked by the progeny of a lesser Gandhi!

SALUTE - Narendra Modi :

Salute to Narendra Modi, TALLEST Leader Narendra Modi being overtaken by Rishi Sunak of the UK in IMPORTANCE among Hindus at Global Level?

Gandhi became a great person of India through the policy of falsehood of "Non-Violence" killing millions of Indians and displacing the millions by the division of India, Modi became popular after the Godra incident and Gujarat Rioting but not a great humanitarian like Abraham Lincoln, who had united the country to form the Superpower the USA or like Naeopolian, who brought the Rule of "Democracy". Modi can influence Putin or Binden of American President but failed to win over Pakistan PM Imran Khan. Political power can be achieved by the act of politics but becoming a humanitarian requires universal love, love for all people, irrespective of Hindu Muslim, or any kind of sectarianism.

Q.No17 - What was the personal motive of Mahatma Gandhi in India in the freedom struggle?

The myth that the European powers were in a hurry to get out of colonization after WW2 — is so stupid. In fact, once the dust of WW2 settled, the European powers were as eager to continue with their empires.

Look at Vietnam for instance. The French were thoroughly humiliated in WW2. That didn't stop them from fighting for their key colony after the war. That started the Vietnam War in which the Americans later got foolishly involved. For decades after WW2, the Vietnamese struggled to get the west off their back. Only in the 1970s did Vietnam get real independence. Indochina Wars.

In the same way, the Dutch who were weaker than the French tried to continue their occupation in Indonesia. It involved a bloody armed conflict — Indonesian National Revolution — to get the Dutch packed off from Indonesia in 1949.

It took a lot of war and violence to get Portugal out of Angola, Goa, East Timor and elsewhere. As late as the 1970s, the Portuguese were fighting to retain their colonies, Angolan War of Independence. And that too it ended only when there was a coup to overthrow the regime in Portugal.

And the British were not to be left behind. They allied with the French to keep the colonisation of the Suez canal, - Suez Crisis. It took a brutal rebellion to get them to exit Kenya in the 1950s [Mau Mau Uprising]. By the time they quit Zimbabwe it was 1980.

All of these in spite of the NAM pushing hard in the UN to decolonize. All of this in spite of the USSR tacitly powering the rebels in the colonies.

Dozens of other examples are there. Suffice to say that European powers were in no mood to give up their colonies after WW2. And none of these colonies were as lucrative as India. Nobody would quit that voluntarily just because they lost a war.

In INDIA We have hundreds of idiotic groups hating Mahatma Gandhi for their own reasons. Jingoist Englishmen hated Gandhi as he was a nationalist Indian. Jingoistic Indians hate Gandhi for being friendly to the UK. Extremist Muslims and Sikhs hate him because he is a Hindu. Extremist Hindus hate him because he was "not Hindu enough" [according to their own random logic]. For Communists, he was a capitalist. For capitalists, he was a communist. Upper castes hate him for being friendly with the Dalits. Dalits hate him for being friendly with the upper castes.

Try loving everyone and you get hated by most. Ironically, the Hindus, Sikhs, Muslims, Christians, neo-buddhists everyone stand united in hating the Mahatma. They don't agree on anything else!

Bose, Patel and other great Indians dotted Gandhi. It was Bose who titled Gandhi as "Father of the Nation". Patel treated Gandhi like a guru. And the alleged fans of Patel and Bose hating Gandhi is tragically ironic.

Oh, India's independence was for all practical purposes decided well before the INA trials [Simla Conference]. Only a few sticky items like Dominion status vs. full sovereignty were discussed. An empire doesn't quit just because some rebels threatened mutiny. They have seen far worse and would put down far worse rebellions.

Assume whatever factors consider, but the fact doesn't change that colonization by Europe didn't end with

WW2. There were decades of brutal repression on many colonies and it took a lot of sacrifice to build the world we are in.

Politics of India is guided by few people who are cunning and power mongers.

Bengal was important during the independence movement where the prominent leader Gandhi succeeded to divide Bengal. Now again after 70 years, the Election of Bengal became an important election-why? Is it for the reunion of Bengal?

Union or Reunion is a natural issue. The objective of the nation is to live in peace and prosperity. The UK united the Islands and made economic prosperity that is why the UK is a great country even though it is a small country with respect to area and population. Thus for the prosperity of Bengalis if the reunion is good, nothing wrong in it.

Prime Minister Nehru had not taken India on Socialist leaning path because it was the easy choice, but because he did not see any other way. Prime Minister Nehru may have been wrong, but really what other choice did he have at that time, this is hard for many to understand today. India in 1947, did not have a skilled labor force, most of the country barely could eat one square meal a day. There was wealth but it was only found with a small percentage of the population and even then, there was not enough capital to build heavy industries to bring India into the 20th century.

People today think India was far more capable than it was then. We talk about how India lacks progress and that our healthcare system is atrocious, that India is not clean nor like a developed nation.

Well in 1947, India was a nation which could not perform basic surgeries in most places. It was a nation where for most people there was no way to educate their children and where a person could perish for lack of basic medicine if they had no money. It was that nation where the elderly man pulled the rickshaw out of the age of colonialism into the age of the new.

In 1916, when Mahatma Gandhi came back to India from South Africa. India was the world's largest poor nation. It had gone from the world's largest exporter of manufactured goods in 1757, to a nation which could not even manufacture its own clothes under British Colonial Rule. Mahatma Gandhi who had once worn Western Style Suits and had a successful career as a barrister, saw that his nation did not share a similar fate at all. For after addressing a session of the Indian National Congress, he vanished to see and find India.

When he returned some years later to the center of the Pan-Indian World, he had traveled in nearly every village in India. He had seen unregulated interest being charged to the poorest in India. He had seen starvation and suffering which was beyond human endurance to bear. He had seen Indians sentenced without fair trials, and others who vanished for expressing desires for home rule. Mahatma Gandhi had seen a nation which had fallen so far below what defines human dignity in even its lowest form. M.K. Gandhi before 1916.

The Indian Freedom Struggle began before Mahatma Gandhi, but Modern Indian Freedom began with Mahatma Gandhi. He showed a path where non-violent resistance could be used more effectively than any forcible resistance. For at the end of the day, there are only two forces which define Empires and these are Economics and Control. Without cooperation neither can function.

So many today in India seem to wish to negate what Mahatma Gandhi accomplished, for they see partition and India's age of innocence and closed economic growth which ended in 1962 and 1992 respectively as having damaged India. But in all reality these two ages were beyond necessary. Pakistan obtained freedom, because of the Indian Freedom Movement not because of Jinnah but in-spite of him. But it did not have the following age of an economic closure and forced Self-Reliance that India had. Today, the difference between India and Pakistan is this very factor. For India took a democratic path no matter how difficult it was, and made the best of it. It closed its economy and built whatever it could with technical assistance initially but with the goal of complete goal of "Swantantrata" or "Self Realization and Self Reliance", this was Mahatma Gandhi's vision.

Prime Minister Nehru did not want India to spend its resources on building a military, and he wanted to help those who were the most vulnerable in society. He thought that the uplift of both India and China was possible based on our shared history and Great Interchange which had lasted for 1500 years before the Islamic Invasion of India. These dreams were shattered when China attacked India in 1962. But, his concept was not wrong. And today, slowly China will have no choice but to embrace peace with India and accept coexistence as a necessity. Prime Minister Nehru's Asian century did not come into existence in the 20th Century but shall now.

The Elderly man pulling the Rickshaw will finally end, and by the middle of this century the dignity that Mahatma Gandhi had envisioned for all Indians and people who were colonized and racially discriminated against will be a thing of the past in great part. For India and China are today the largest investors in many parts of Africa. Ultimately the vision of a man, who gave up all worldly pleasures for a vision of human dignity, opportunity and an end to suffering and starvation, who did not rest but instead tirelessly tread across India, in sweltering heat, rains and oppression. He did not leave wealth nor numbered bank accounts to his family, nor did he offer them greater opportunities than for others. Instead he gave everything he had including his life so that a nation could be free after 190 years of racial, economic and political deprivation rarely seen in history. His cause would become a global cause which still lives on. Mahatma Gandhi, will be remembered for untold generations to come. But still he can not get hold of the DIVISION of the country.

Q.No 18 - What were the important factors that caused the rift between Gandhi and Subhas Chandra Bose?

Gandhi getting failure in the practise of law, involved in the falsehood of "Non-Violence" to make himself great, on the other hand Subhas Chandra Bose, getting excited by the spirit of love for the country and excited to say the Indians "Give me blood, I would give you freedom" which was dead against of Gandhi's slow -gone of "Non-Violence". That was the reason for the rift between Gandhi and Subhas Chandra Bose.

Politics of India is guided by few people who are cunning and power mongers. **Who is the alternative to Narendra Modi in BJP for 2024?**

India is a country of more than hundred cotes. It is not good for anybody to become the PM of india. Another person should get the opportunity to become the PM and try his best to do good for the country.

Q.No. 19 - What is the connection of Subhas Chandra Bose with Jagadish Chandra Bose, Satyendra nath Bose and Amar Bose?

Subash Chandra Bose was no other than Netaji, who thought for India to be liberated by Azaid-Hind-Fauz and make it a country of humanity, a country of Super-power. Sir Jagadish Chandra Bose was a scientist. Again Satyendranath Bose was a student of Jagadish Chandra Bose, he worked with Sir Albert Einstein on quantum mechanics and Amar Bose was an electrical engineer who worked in Massachusetts institute in USA – all were the pride of Bengals but not like present Bengal leaders who hoarded money in cores in Flats after Flats.

Q.No. 20 - What has been done by the WB government to honour Subhas Chandra Bose in the last 15 years?

Nothing but fighting for Chair. Dr. S P Mukherjee became a fool in the name of "Hindu-Bengal". He finally got nothing but the death penalty inside the jail of Kashmir. Bengal was destroyed by Gandhi first by "Non-Violence "and then by division. Poverty prevailed everywhere in Bengal. CPM as the champion of the poor ruled for about 35 years destroying industry, the new Trinomial further destroyed Nano-Industry, came to power and collected huge money by illegal means to purchase vote and thought for power only and had no time or intention to think for Netaji or the people.

Q.No. 21 - Why did Gandhi heavily favor Muslims over Hindus?

E.g.

(1) KHILAFAT MOVEMENT

Yeah, It all started before Independence of India. Mahatma Gandhi was the first person who Started **Muslim**

appeasement in India. Now what is this KHILAFAT Movement ?

During the colonial period the Turkish and Ottoman empire lost the battle. In Islam Khalifa is the most superior person. Every Muslim in the entire world must obey his orders. So Indian Muslims started campaigning for Khalifa and Gandhi supported them. So appeasement started from here.

Now the question arises Why Gandhi favored Muslims over Hindus ?

Gandhi was opposing two nation theory initially. Later he supported it because Nehru was like Son to him. His look out was how to bring Nehru in the forefront but not Jinnah. So Gandhi wanted to collaborate with Muslim league. He even offered reservations for Muslims in parliamentary elections. Mohammad Jinnah wanted to become the first Prime Minister of India which was not in his thinking. So Gandhi was supporting Nehru. Partition happened, Jinnah went to Pakistan and Nehru became the PM of India.

Why did Gandhi unite Hindus and Muslims?

He did not unite, he just encouraged the formation of Muslim League by his appeasement policies that led to the massacre of millions. All Gandhi did was blackmail Hindus into listening to him by his "fasts unto death" that, unlike Bhagat Singh, never led to death.

Q.No. 22 - Is Mahatma Gandhi responsible for the India-Pakistan division?

Gandhi and Nehru (his political successor and protege) had neither the political acumen to see into the future nor the will to implement a grand vision for India and their non-violent puritanism was actually a very inhibiting factor in nation-building in 1947.

Patel was much more astute and savvy in these matters and had a very good grasp of Realpolitik.

EU also might face this situation in the next few years where burgeoning Muslim populations in the EU may start attacking and terrorizing Europeans to give them a separate Islamic State in Southern Europe (Spain)

So this process of Pakistanization which was successful in the case of India in the year 1947, is not just restricted to that unfortunate country alone.

It can even happen in China if the population of Uighurs reaches 33% of the Chinese population or Australia or South Africa if Muslims population in these countries reaches 33% of the total population.

It is also started in Indian Kashmir (where Kashmiri Pandits have been chased out of their homeland) by Islamist fanatics sponsored by Pakistan.

Now let me draw some parallels to the US civil war where Americans had to face a similar nation-fracturing phase..in their history.

If we go over the US-Civil war history in the US, there was no third party like the British involved. The Americans were the captains of their own destiny with no power like the British overseeing the civil war.

Another historic fact one needs to consider is that the British were preoccupied with and exhausted after the Sepoy rebellion in India which broke out in 1857, and had just concluded a few years before the outbreak of the American Civil War.

This prevented the British from siding with the Southern-Secessionist-Slave states against the Northern Unionist-Free States in the US Civil War of 1861-65.

Lincoln, who was the president at that time, emphatically declared in his famous: Lincoln's House Divided Speech A house divided against itself cannot stand. He believed this government cannot endure, permanently, half slave and half free. He did not expect the Union to be dissolved

Jefferson Davis - who was the equivalent of a Jinnah in the US, and President of the Southern Secessionist States, decided to split the US into two countries in 1861 and attacked the Northern states who were in favor of the Union and abolition of Slavery all over the US.

Three years after making his speech, Lincoln was not afraid of waging a brutal war to preserve the Union, even if it meant the use of maximum force, strategy and violence which resulted in the deaths of tens of thousands of fellow Americans who fought bitterly for the Secessionist Southern states which supported slavery.

In the case of the US, the Unionists had a crushing victory over the secessionists in 1865 and the Union of the United States was preserved and this allowed theAmericans to become the world power that it is today.

Unfortunately, for India, and the Indian people, they had a leader whose rigid convictions prevented him from indulging in a war to prevent the partition of India, nor did the person whom he appointed as his political successor -Nehru who was a weakling, a Pacifist and an active proponent of "non-violence" himself, have the stomach for a quick war which if he had mobilized the

Indian people and launched in 1951, would have settled the matter in 1954 itself.

So it was a fact that India and the Indian people were unfortunate on both counts in this nascent phase of their history.

b) The British - who never had the interests of the Indian peoples in their hearts and minds and did everything in their power to support the partition of the Indian homeland and undermine the Indians.

The British hated the idea of having to give up possession of their prize colony India in 1947.

Also Britain which was economically devastated after World War II wanted to use this inter-state rivalry between the two newly created states in the Indian subcontinent to sell weapons to both countries and benefit from this sales of weapons to boost their crippled economy.

Many of the Indians are the hard critics of Mahatma Gandhi during the days of college life. Many Indians heartly liked the revolutionary youth like Bhagat Singh, Azad. It was because he used to think this was the only way to liberate India from colonialism. The British were selfish, egoistic with white-superiority, They didn't have inner conscience to see the deprived ones of famines and starving Indians.

The other point of contention with Gandhian ideology was that it was at confrontation with Subash Chandra Bose views. A visionary could know about Gandhian Vision, methods to achieve the vision and the comprehensive nature of Gandhi as a leader making himself a global leader by the mischievous method of treasury.

So clever he was when many will realize why the Greatest Scientist of the time, Albert Einstein dedicated a few soothing words to Gandhi

Thereby Gandhi became a Global leader and Gandhi became virtually a 'virtual Godfather' for many. Now, slowly things are getting exposed whereby all the highlights of all dimensions of Gandhi, which led the world once to bow against Gandhian Ideology, is going to expose the right way leading him to the worst creature of humanity.

On the other hand he tried to be a **global leader**, He raised voices against racism-white superiority in Africa, fought for equal rights for brothers from other Motherland and dedicated his desire for human rights conservation. Many British colonies stood against discriminatory nature of the empire. Far later Martin Luther King Jr. and Nelson Mandela drew their inspiration from the successful experiments of Gandhi. Gandhi appealed to Adolf Hilter to restore global peace at the start of World War-2, but Hilter ignored Gandhi's advice, rest is known to the world.

He raised his voice against violations of human rights in China, Burma and other imperial colonies. It was the legacy for Gandhian Foreign Policy that Nehru extended as Non-Aligned Movement (NAM).

The global community loves and respects Gandhi for his **Visionary Ideology**for India and methods to achieve them. Gandhian Ideology became very vast and comprehensive in nature.

Gandhi landed India in 1915 and his first wish was to decode the Real India, analyze reasons for colonialism and grass root problems of India. He visited villages, districts until his first experiment on Indian soil i.e. Champaran Satyagraha. He concluded that Union Jack was powerful enough that many technologically advanced, militarily superior and economically sound nations were under the shadow of British imperialism. The British were artists of divide and rule theory, they knew the art of cropping feud in a society. A majorly illiterate, but diverse and pluralistic society like India was an ideal place to perform the acid tests of the British Arts.

They have tight control over all wings of government- Judiciary, Administration, Police, Legislature. Congressmen were disillusioned with Swaraj. So, any revolutionary attempt could have given you a temporary edge over the British, but the repercussions would have been suffered by the peasants in the form of high taxation, by common citizens through Black Act (Rowlatt Act), punitive detention and a series of tortures on innocent protesters. Gandhi wanted to hit at the base of British strategy through **'Unite and Protest' against 'Divide and Rule'**. He knew that any movement has its life and it cannot be for a long time because, practically people have a responsibility to feed the starving family. A prolonged movement would hit the wages and productivity of Indians, which no one can refund. Gandhi was pragmatic in approach. He came up with the same weapons of non-violence (to avoid atrocities after any repercussions of protest), communal harmony (NCM-Khilafat joint movement for Hindu-Muslim Unity), social integration (fight against untouchability to consolidate Hindus).

His clear principles can be analysed through his statements that he was a supporter of the 'Varna Ashram' system of Vedas, but disregard untouchability. He was neutral to both higher and lower castes, he didn't want to appease a particular section but desired 'one nation, one society':- a totally different feature from current political leadership (Look at Owaisi sahab, Yogi Baba, Behan Ji, Netaji).

Whatever we generally read or view on TV about Gandhi is the political dimension of Gandhian ideology. We all know about his successful Satyagraha in South Africa and the same success in India. But mere Independence was never a vision of Gandhi. He wanted a citizenry with high moral values of truth, non-violence and fraternity.

Just Imagine if India had heard his preaching of non-violence in Noakhali and Delhi, we don't have to go for surgical and air strikes on Pakistan. I don't mean that there would be no partition at all. Gandhi knew that partition was inevitable because his last attempts to avoid partition, through asking Nehru to give ruling power to Jinnah and request to Mount batten to convince both parties, proved to be failures. He was totally broken from inside.

He had a vow of silence on 15th August 1947, the greatest day of celebrations at both sides of Wagah- Attari Border. All that he desired after the failed persuasion were- communal understanding and a peaceful partition. If India was divided peacefully, We wouldn't have any animosity with Pakistanis. But since we still have a pre-independent generation in our society who have a long list of losses of loved lives and detachment from homelands, which are main reasons for grief and animosity for our neighboring nation. Post-liberalization generations don't have enough issues with Pakistan, beside the Kargil war and habitual infiltration, which too has roots in the partition period of bloodshed.

Citizens didn't have enough fault in 1946–47, it was political leadership at both sides that ignored Gandhi and misguided people completely to enthrone themselves in their respective nations. After 7 decades of both nations, we can easily evaluate the social and economic progress of both. The world just laughs at both of the countries India-Pakistan.

We are forgetting his words, so here are we as a global community:- Inward-looking economies with migration and refugees crisis, radicalism, terrorism, raising questions on our fellow Muslim friends, labeling dissent as anti-national, intensively hating a nation that stands no where with us in economics and defense spectra.

World respects Gandhi (Example- 2nd October was designated as International Non-violence Day unanimously by all United Nations members), but it's our time to follow Gandhi in letter and spirit. To put this in Gandhian Words- "We have to be vigilant to ourselves, the change should come from conscience, forceful changes are temporary". Gandhi had a comprehensive and practical vision for upcoming generations of both the nations, but no one listened to him. Today, when we are moving ahead to celebrate his 150th birth anniversary, we need an introspection. An introspection as an individual, as a society and as a nation. An introspection with confession, that how much we have followed the most loved global figure of truth, intolerance and non-violence

Q.No. 23 - How did secularism and non violence of Gandhi destroy India?

These are two Gandhian political tools utilized by the Congress party for its existence for the last 70 years. In the name of secularism Congress played vote bank politics. Secondly, Congress marketed non violence in the name of Gandhi and won sympathy from voters as if Congress is following Gandhiji's agenda.

In foreign policy, Congress pursued weak diplomacy with neighbors particularly with China and Chinese took maximum advantage of our weakness and captured Tibet and occupied large tracts of our territories illegally and till today we are unable to recover the same from them. Tibet is permanently lost.

In respect of Pakistan, we gave so much scope to them for peaceful co-existence however Pakistanis ultimately misused our friendliness by troubling us with intermittentterrorism in the country.

The Indian Army was not fully developed with modern warfare and whenever we wanted to purchase Arms from advanced countries, they hired commission agencies to loot money in the name of armaments.

So both secularism and Nonviolence were misused for political gains by Congress.

Q.No. 24 - Why was India divided on religious lines?

For the congress Rule to rule India forever with the Gandhi Family! If India is not divided on Religious lines, Gandhi is not required for India. Gandhi fought for the Muslim rights more than freedom actually! So to counter

Gandhi at that time, some Hindus were forced to Polarize on the basis of Religion and created Hindu Mahasabha!

And the British were the first to invent that Dividing India on Religious lines is the easiest way to Rule Whole India! And the Nehru Family copied this concept and ruled Independent India Very easily!

Jawaharlal Nehru and Indira Gandhi did not agree to even reasonable demands of Hindus during their rule. Still Hindus were electing them to power with a high majority. Why?

It was because Hindus were fools, and dark in religion because of cowardness. They never learn how to live together, because they are selfish, they like to love themselves. They were greedy. They sacrificed their 12-year-old girl to 70-year-old Brahmins to marry, and burn-in a funeral along with her old husband for the greediness of future pleasure in heaven. In Hindu India, there were more than 500 hundred princely states but not in unity because of selfish character. They don't know how to rule and how to live with all in unity.

Q.No. 25 - What factors caused Mahatma Gandhi to come to India?

A saint's invite anticipated Gandhi when he arrived on January 9, 1915, at the Apollo Bunder in Bombay. After three days he was regarded by the individuals of Bombay at a heavenly gathering in the palatial place of a Bombay head honcho Jehangir Petit. The Government of India got together with the individuals of India in showering praises on Gandhi. He got a "Kaiser-I-Hind '' gold award in the King's birthday praises rundown of 1915. His relationship with Gokhale ensured enough of his being a sheltered government official. Obviously, he had driven an extra-sacred development in South Africa, challenged laws and filled goals, however the reason for which he had battled showed up as much philanthropic as political, dear to all Indian as and all Englishmen whose feeling of mankind had not been blunted by racial haughtiness or political convenience. Ruler Hardinge's open help of the Satyagraha development had expelled the shame of defiance from South Africa's Indian development.

Gandhi was in no rush to drive into governmental issues. His political tutor on the Indian scene was Gokhale. One of the principal things Gokhale did was to separate a guarantee from Gandhi that he would not communicate upon open inquiries for a year, which was to be a "time of probation". Gokhale was extremely sharp that Gandhi should join the Servants of India Society in Poona. Gandhi was very much ready to fall in with the desires of Gokhale, however a few individuals from the Society expected that there was too incredible a hole between the goals and techniques for the Society and those of Gandhi. While the topic of his confirmation as a 'Worker of India' was being discussed, Gandhi visited the places where he grew up of Porbandar and Rajkot and went on to Shantiniketan in West Bengal, the cosmopolitan University of the Poet Rabindranath Tagore.

The excursion to Shantiniketan finished unexpectedly with a wire from Poona that Gokhale was dead. Gandhi was dazed. He grieved Gokhale by going shoeless for a year, and keeping in mind the memory of his guide, put forth another attempt to look for admission to the Servants of India Society. Finding a sharp division of supposition in the Society on this point, he pulled back his application for affirmation.

During 1915—the time of probation—Gandhi shunned legislative issues harshly. In his discourses and compositions he limited himself to the change of the individual and the general public and stayed away from the issues which ruled Indian governmental issues. His limitation was incompletely because of deliberate quietness and somewhat to the way that he was all the while considering conditions in India and deciding.

Q.No. 26 - Is Mahatma Gandhi responsible for the India-Pakistan division? or--What is this whole process of the creation of Pakistan... ?

In respect of a clear answer to this question, one has to see it as an Indian-Civil-War which is still ongoing and now has an added nuclear dimension to it.

To a large extent Gandhi was responsible for this unhappy state of affairs in the Indian subcontinent, because he did not do enough to prevent it or was hidebound by his rigid convictions to think outside the box - of different ways to prevent it.

As such Gandhi and Nehru (his political successor and protege) had neither the political acumen to see into the future nor the will to implement a grand vision for India and their non-violent puritanism was actually a very inhibiting factor in nation-building in 1947.

Patel was much more astute and savvy in these matters and had a very good grasp of Real politics.

Honestly, a real devoted public servant can explain it better in the following impartial manner.

If Muslims were/are a sizable minority in any country, even in the USA, UK, Australia or Russia for that matter, the process of Pakistanization - or -

"Islamist-Supremacist-Secessionist agitation accompanied by violent struggle and supported by frequent acts of terror against a host nation, for the establishment of a separate Islamic country in a host nation"

---------- is very much a possibility.

EU may face this situation in the next few years where burgeoning Muslim populations in the EU may start attacking and terrorizing Europeans to give them a separate Islamic State in Southern Europe (Spain)

So this process of Pakistanization which was successful in the case of India in the year 1947, is not just restricted to that unfortunate country alone.

It can even happen in China if the population of Uighurs reaches 33% of the Chinese population or Australia or South Africa if Muslims population in these countries reaches 33% of the total population.

For the record it is happening in Indian Kashmir (where Kashmiri Pandits have been chased out of their homeland) by Islamist fanatics sponsored by Pakistan.

It also happened in the US civil war where Americans had to face a similar nation-fracturing phase..in their history.

If we go over the US-Civil war history in the US, there was no third party like the British involved. Another historic fact one needs to consider is that the British were preoccupied with and exhausted after the Sepoy rebellion in India which broke out in 1857, and had just concluded a few years before the outbreak of the American Civil War.

Lincoln was not afraid of waging a brutal war to preserve the Union, even if it meant the use of maximum force, strategy and violence which resulted in the deaths of tens of thousands of fellow Americans who fought bitterly for the Secessionist Southern states which supported slavery.

In the case of the US, the Unionists had a crushing victory over the secessionists in 1865 and the Union of the United States was preserved and this allowed Americans to become the world power today.

Unfortunately, for India, and the Indian people, they had a leader whose rigid convictions prevented him from indulging in a war to prevent the partition of India, nor did the person whom he appointed as his political successor -Nehru who was a weakling, a Pacifist and an active proponent of "non-violence" himself, have the stomach for a quick war which if he had mobilized the Indian people and launched in 1951, would have settled the matter in 1954 itself.

Moreover, Pakistan was British Premier Winston Churchill's pet idea and was fully supported by first the British and later the American governments who at that time, had the idea of using Pakistan to contain Soviet expansionism South, towards the warmer waters of the Arabian Sea during the Cold war.

In the case of INDIA (a) a bad or weak leader like Gandhi who did not have the foresight to see the problems which would have stranded the subcontinent and still continue to do so today by allowing Pakistan to be formed and also acquire Nuclear weapons

and

(b)**An inimical overseeing power:** The British - who never had the interests of the Indian peoples in their hearts and minds and did everything in their power to support the partition of the Indian homeland and undermine the Indians.

The British hated the idea of having to give up possession of their prize colony India in 1947. (India being the primary reason Britain had gained world power status in the 19th and early 20th Centuries) and their parting gift or rather (kick) to the Indian people was this artificial-partition of the Indian homeland and the horrendous violence and unnecessary migrations which accompanied it.

Also Britain which was economically devastated after World War II wanted to use this inter-state rivalry between the two newly created states in the Indian subcontinent to sell weapons to both countries and benefit from this sales of weapons to boost their crippled economy.

After this if the final Union of India is accomplished, - which is good for India, Pakistan and Bangladesh and ultimately good for the world, the Indians can probably say:

The American civil war lasted 4 years from 1861-1965, ours unfortunately lasted for so many years and finally we were saved by the UNITY.

In short he was very clever, he made Nehru the PM for his self image and kicked away the powerful intelligent Muslim Leader Jinnah by the DIVISION OF INDIA. Even by his religious attachment he could not allow the two times elected President Subhas to function in the Congress. From the activity of my personal life I could know and judge GANDHI better. Let me write something about myself and how to know Gandhi a little better.

Author had the opportunity to go to England to know the mystery of science, where he had the opportunity to know the little country UK, their activity in administration and imparting education for the nation where our leader Gandhi got the opportunity to study Law. However, I turned my attention to SCIENCE to become a research worker to UMIST (UK), and later to become a professor of UMIST, return to my country to serve the nation, and later become an advocate to study the laws of the land, the know the reason of the poor conditions of the people in compare to western life. In INDIA most of the politicians were busy with how to capture power and money by exploiting the common people in the name of the betterment of the nation. If there be anybody at the top, who is no other than the Great Gandhi, who had no other skill except the orthodox religion, although he had a law degree from Inner Temple, although he tried to practice law at Bombay, but was a complete failure, rescued by Motilal Nehru, for his son J. Nehru who never hesitated to divide the country as he was a coward politician, no parallel with Jinnah, removed Jinnah with secret understanding by dividing the county bringing Nehru in front, who had been made a politician, who had no political IQ except the sexy life with Mountbatten and many other Girls, like the so called Saint Gandhi, what is known to everyone, how he could bath with beautiful girl, how he could sleep naked with two girls in spite of objection from his close associates in Sabarmati Ashram.

The secret pact, made a foolish, sexy, luxurious wealthy son (by dint of Father's property, contributing zero, unlike Jinnah & Jinnah house) Nehru the PM to make himself the FATHER of the nation and by Nehru's patronage he became an International ICON of peace subsiding the killing of millions Punjabis and Bengalis and displacing the millions. If Gandhi is called the greatest enemy of humanity, it would be less. Killing people is BARBARISM, and everywhere it is done with heroism, Abraham Lincoln killed millions of people with heroic Barbarism for which USA today is a super power, Barbarism continued in French, for which democracy was established in the France after French Revolution. Gandhi carried out cowardice, the worst kind of wicked Barbarism in the name of "non-Violence" taking the advantage of Hindu Bengali's religious weakness and foolishness to destroy the common people particularly in Bengali of Bengal subjecting them to kill in famine after famine just to make name and fame for himself acting as a secret agent of British.

The aim was to capture power somehow, let the country go to hell. It is now even after 70 years that INDIANS could see Hindu-Muslim Mujaffarabad being the worst kind of rioting where little children were killed and died. Is it Gandhi's rightful honor to be a man of peace, rather a man of killer for name and fame ever born in the UNIVERSE? Now the last wish of all INDIANS is to see a corruption free India under Modi, and a country of one nation with one Indian identity before the death of all INDIANS.

Gandhi was the destroyer of India by division of India on the basis of religion and B.R. Ambedkar, an educated short sighted Dalit lawyer, was the destroyer of India by dividing the Indians on the basis of castes outlined in the constitution for reservation instead of reservation for economically backward sections of the society.

All these leaders were short sighted and worked for self interest. Gandhi having being a Inner Temple Barrister brought religion in a clever way designing himself a saint with a half naked Fakir Dress just to be-fool the common Hindu religious minded people to accomplish his secret mission of bringing Nehru in the chair of PM and placing himself in the post of icon without caring the common Indians. Today even after 70 years Indians are facing Hindu-Muslim rioting because of Gandhi and now people are fighting among themselves with Dali-NonDalit because of the short sighted leader like B.R.Ambedkar.

It is nothing but foolishness not to talk with Pakistan. Who were Pakistanis? They were our brothers and sisters. All were born and brought up in India. It is only a belief of Islam that has originated in Arab Land that has been spread here. But how can a brother be a no-brother? It was only Gandhi, a selfish cowardly person who brought the difference between Hindus and Muslims of Indians through the ethics of "NON-VIOLENCE" for his own image by removing efficient Jinnah and bringing foolish Nehru into the Chair.

Let us write again to remind the INDIANS that it is nothing but foolishness not to talk with Pakistan. Who were Pakistanis? They were our brothers and sisters.

All were born and brought up in India. It is only a belief of Islam that has originated in Arab Land that has been spread here. But how can a brother be a no-brother? It was only Gandhi, a selfish cowardly person who brought the difference between Hindus and Muslims of Indians through the ethics of "NON-VIOLENCE" for his own image by removing efficient Jinnah and bringing foolish Nehru into the Chair.

A better destiny of East Bengal Hindus lies in the UNITY of two Bengal : If India and Pakistan are able to settle all their differences amicably, who will be the biggest loser and who will be the biggest winner in such a scenario? No one is but the Indian people.

It was Gandhi who was the destroyer of India by confirming the division of India as Hindu, Muslim. Once all were Indians in the Indian subcontinent although they remained and ruled under princely STATES. All are human beings of Indian soil with the same food, custom and nature. They will be happy only when they live together, forgetting all kinds of rivalry. It was realized by Jinnah before the end of his life for which Jinnah said, in his dying bed, that the greatest blunder he made was by dividing India.

If India and Pakistan are able to settle all their differences amicably, who will be the biggest loser and who will be the biggest winner in such a scenario? It is only INDIANS.

It is again "No one is but the Indian people". It was Gandhi who was the destroyer of India by confirming the division of India as Hindu, Muslim. Once all were Indians. All are human beings of Indian soil with the same food, custom and nature. They will be happy only when they live, forgetting all kinds of rivalry. Rabridra & Nazrul are the souls of Bengalis, their soul lives in the United Bengal.

Q. No28- Why was Winston Churchill so popular with the British people, and why is he still considered one of the greatest leaders in history?

Unlike GANDHI, **Winston Churchill** was the greatest thinker for the BRITISH PEOPLE, in spite of the downfall of the FRENCH, who saved the people of UK from the warrior Hitler by his forceful voice of "Encouragement" to his obedient BRITISH Soldiers un like GANDHI, who agreed to surrender to militant FORCE of JINNAH in view of the massacre of CALCUTTA KILLING of 16th AUGUST, 1946.

Winston Churchill saved the UK from the bombing on the slaughter of Hitler without surrender while Indian Leader Gandhi surrendered to Jinnah and agreed to partition India due to "CALCUTT KILLING" due to 2% Muslim Militant of INDIA. Who will not say GANDHI was the destroyer of beautiful UNITED INDIA.

World War II was the design of Hitler. The military ruler Hitler of Germany became a threat to other nations of Europe, because of the strength of the military. But Churchill never dared to express his resentment against Hitler in British Parliament. By 1938, as Germany began its occupation in controlling its neighbors, Churchill had become a staunch critic of British Prime Minister Neville Chamberlain's policy of appeasement toward the Nazis. In 1938 Chamberlain returned from Munich proclaiming "peace for our time" after sacrificing Czechoslovakia to Hitler, Churchill was furious.

Germany very soon unilaterally occupied the vital Norwegian iron mines and sea ports. It was in a debate in parliament on the Norwegian crisis that led to a vote of no confidence toward Prime Minister Chamberlain. By May 1940, Britain and her allies were losing the war. In the face of the Nazis' relentless march across Europe, Chamberlain bowed to pressure and resigned as prime minister. In no time King George VI appointed Churchill as prime minister and minister of defense.

Immediately the German army began its Western offensive, invading the Netherlands, Belgium, and Luxembourg. Hitler invaded Poland on 1 September 1939. Britain was once again at war with Germany.

On 3rd September 1939, the day that Britain declared war on Germany.

Hitler could not tolerate the declaration of aggression of the French and Britain. Two days later, Hitler applied his war skills and allowed the forces to enter France. Britain stood alone against the onslaught. Quickly, in order to form a unity among all, Churchill formed a coalition cabinet consisting of leaders from the Labor, Liberal, and Conservative parties and led the country to face war by placing intelligent and talented men in positions.

In 1940, Winston Churchill became the prime minister of Britain. He was successful in leading a successful Allied strategy with the United States and Russia. France.

Now standing alone, Churchill's speeches stirred Britain to continue fighting until the US and Russia joined the war in 1941. On 6June, 1944, US, British and Canadian forces invaded Nazi –occupied. D-Day had arrived.

More than 150,000 troops landed on French soil in the biggest ever seaborne invasion. On 7 May 1945, Germany surrendered, Though Japan would continue fighting until September, and the Allies had won. Churchill had led the nation to Victory.

If we look at the performance of GANDHI we could see, a poor fellow was begging for everything without any ability, without any determination. Winston Churchill saved the nation from the point of collapse under the bombing stroke of Hitler keeping the nation hanging for more than a year while the weak leader Gandhi claiming the leader of more than 100 million people of India did not have a mental stamina to keep the nation at least for few months but not to surrender to watch the situation to save the nation from disaster or breaking into pieces. Will his performance make **the Indians brave and proud?**

There is no doubt that the INDIAN leader GANDHI is an inhuman creature compared to Winston Churchill but he is even worse than Hitler. Let us see

GANDHI VS Adolf Hitler:

Adolf Hitler could not win the war, but he had made the people happy and proud by his double stroke action.

By one as in the Economic Front, he was successful in overcoming depression and to make people happy by reducing the rate of unemployment from six million in 1932 to one million in 1936, by second in the warfront he fought for justice making the Germans great and sacrificed the life for the nation although he was defeated.

On the other hand **Mohandas Karamchand Gandhi** in the Economic Front could not remove the famine situation, due to which lakhs of people died in Bengal, and on the rioting front as good as the warfront, he could not save the killings of millions, but finally agreed to the demand of division with humiliation making the country men unhappy, making himself a victim of bullet. Who is the man dearest to the country with honour and dignity, **Gandhi or Hitler?**

Q.No. 29 - Why were differences between Mahatma Gandhi and Bhimrao Ambedkar?

Both were self centered and selfish people. Gandhi tried to increase his image by making Nehru the PM of India while Ambedkar tried to increase his image by keeping reservations for his own community. Both were working against the UNITY and PROSPERITY of India. So both were the real destroyers of Great INDIA.

Q.No. 30 - Why were some freedom fighters not given any award by their government?

The people in the government very well knew that they did nothing for the country except something for the self image and something to attain power. Nobody dared to give any prize exceptNetaji but the activity of Netaji was totally against the falsehood movement of "NON-VIOLENCE". Everybody is conscious of the Hindu - Muslim Rioting because of personal achievement.

The Kashmiri massacre was due to Hindu-Muslim Religion. Who brought religion into politics? It was Gandhi. Why? To increase his name and fame through the falsehood of "Non-Violence" a movement of "AHINGSA". Is it ahingsa?

So Gandhi's name must be vanished from India and like RUSSIA who did once vanished so many religious people like Gandhi for the betterment of Russia.

Q.No. 31 - Was Mohandas Karamchand Gandhi a good man or a bad man? Why?

The British Empire made Gandhi popular around the world due to his Non Violence Movement which worked in British favor and Gandhi loved and enjoyed this recognition and began favoring British Rule indirectly.

Some real life facts about Gandhi:

In 1885, Gandhi's father, Karamchand, developed a fistula and grew gravely ill. One night soon after, according to a 2010 biography, Gandhi was sitting up with his father, but eventually left to have sex with his new bride, Kasturba. Karamchand died while Gandhi was away.

Not long after, he went to South Africa, where perhaps his darkest chapter begins...

He was staunchly racist for at least much of his adulthood.

Before leading his historic push for India's independence from the British Empire, Gandhi famously led civil rights movements in South Africa, another British colony, between 1893 and 1915, when he was in his mid-20s through his mid-40s.

While Gandhi's time fighting for the rights of Indians in South Africa is often now mythologized as the heroic precursor to his later efforts in India, the dark side of this tale reveals that Gandhi's motivations in South Africa included his strident racism against the local black populations there.

He had young girls sleep nude next to him in order to test his chastity.

After Gandhi's father died while Gandhi was off having sex, and once again after coming to the realization that he couldn't serve humanity while also consumed by lust, a thirty-something Gandhi decided that he must take a vow of chastity and tested that chastity in some rather odd ways.

Although he forbade men and women (even husbands and wives) from sleeping together while at his ashrams, Gandhi had many women, some of them teenagers, some of them married, sleep nude in his bed.

His list of nude sleeping partners included his own grandniece.

The year before his death, a 77-year-old Gandhi cast a then 33-year-old Sushila Nayar (who Gandhi had asked to be given to him as a gift by her mother when she was just six) out of his bed in favor of a younger woman: Manu, his 18-year-old grandniece.

Gandhi explicitly stated that sleeping with Manu in the nude yet resisting sexual temptation was his most important experiment in chastity, telling her that:

"[we] must put our purity to the ultimate test."

At that same time, he also pulled Abha, the 18-year-old wife of his grandnephew, into bed with him and things quickly became problematic. When Gandhi began publicly speaking about his sleeping arrangement, even those in his inner circle asked that he remove the girls from his bed. He initially refused; finally, after several of his close associates parted ways with him over the matter, he relented.

Nevertheless, he asked that Manu share their sleeping arrangement with the world once he died. When that happened just months later, however, Gandhi's associates, including his son, made it clear to Manu that she should keep her mouth shut.

He was unusually preoccupied with semen and nocturnal emissions.

Given his extraordinary chastity experiments, Gandhi is on record as being particularly concerned about avoiding any kind of ejaculation.

In describing his philosophy of celibacy, he stated that he strove to be:

"One who never has any lustful intention, who, by constant attendance upon God, has become proof against conscious or unconscious emissions." He thus complained about the nocturnal emissions he suffered and said that, "One who conserves his vital fluid acquires unfailing power."

What's more, he kept none of this to himself, instead making his views on semen and ejaculation part of his sermons, and even asserting that his avoidance of ejaculation was essential in helping India reach independence, stating:

"I hold that the true service of the country demands this observance."

He carried out his sexual experiments with the boys and girls at his ashrams.

While Gandhi clearly had his own, deep-seated sexual hang-ups resulting in fervid chastity and experiments designed to test that chastity, what's more problematic is that he acted out similar experiments with others -- specifically, children.

Although husbands and wives weren't even allowed to sleep together at his ashrams, the boys and girls were -- all under Gandhi's peculiar supervision.

First, they would bathe together:

"I sent the boys reputed to be mischievous and the innocent young girls to bathe at the same time,"

Gandhi said, according to Adams' biography. Then, they would sleep, beds very close together, with Gandhi often there himself to act as a watchdog.

If any of the boys or girls succumbed to temptation -- temptation that Gandhi himself all but orchestrated -- they were punished. And to add insult to injury, it seems that the boys didn't get it as badly as the girls, whose hair would be chopped off if they misbehaved.

He had intimate relationships with many women, young companions aside, other than his wife throughout his life.

Although Gandhi married Kasturba Kapadia in an arranged marriage while teenagers, they stayed together all their lives. Nevertheless, even if Gandhi's needs weren't overtly sexual, they did draw him into many inappropriately intimate relationships with other women (aside from the young girls we've already discussed).

There was Madeleine Slade, the daughter of a British admiral who left home to devote herself to Gandhi and his work. The two were inseparable and exchanged countless intimate missives that, many note, read like love letters.

Then there was Saraladevi Chaudhurani, a Bengali activist to whom he grew very close, inviting her to his ashram and enraging his wife by spending plenty of time alone with her and allowing her to avoid the chores required of everyone else. In a letter to a friend, he once referred to her as his "spiritual wife."

He had some rather cruel things to say about his wife.

Although Gandhi and his wife stayed married their entire lives, it's readily apparent that Gandhi's vows of poverty and chastity drove this once well-to-do couple apart, and that Gandhi felt that his wife was never on the same spiritual and intellectual plane as he. He would go on to say some cruel things about her, including:

"I simply cannot bear to look at Ba's face. The expression is often like that on the face of a meek cow and gives one the feeling as a cow occasionally does, that in her own dumb manner she is saying something."

He was likely responsible for his wife's death.

What's troubling about Gandhi's unusual lifestyle choices, celibacy, poverty, fasting, is that he forced them upon his family as well. By all accounts, his wife managed to put up with these things, but they (namely, the poverty) eventually helped eat away at her health. In early 1944, when she was stricken with pneumonia, Gandhi once again imposed his choices upon her and refused to allow her to be injected with "alien medicine," i.e. penicillin.

Soon after, she died. And not long after that, Gandhi himself contracted malaria. But this time, he allowed doctors to inject him with quinine and save his life.

He was shockingly sexist.

Though plenty of ink has been spilled over Gandhi's supposed feminism, there are just too many facts and stories to the contrary to ignore.

Q.No. 32 - Who were the freedom fighters influenced by Mahatma Gandhi?

The poor village uneducated people who were exploited by the art of religion dressing himself as a half naked FAKIR as good as a great SAINT sent by God from heaven to Earth. The CLEVER GANDHI by dint of his half naked SAINTLY DRESS convinces the poor villagers that they should join the movement of "NON-VIOLENCE" to kick out the BRITISH for the betterment of INDIA and Indian people.

Q.NO. 33 - What and why did Gandhi want Muslims in India when 2 separate nations were given to them?

Gandhi was a clever person. He only knows how to increase his name and fame. He started the "Non-Violence" Movement to satisfy the Indians as well as the British. **Jinnah once said, in the dying bed, that the greatest blunder he made was by dividing India. The set back of the division of British INDIA was realized by Jinnah but no realization was ever noticed on the part of GANDHI, one imagines how inhuman GANDHI was?**

Publicly he exposed himself as a SAINT with a half naked FAKIR Dress fighting for a united independent India. Finding Jinnha's popularity he could not control himself, so he went against all kinds of activity to make himself popular.

Q.No. 34 - How do I write an essay on Mahatma Gandhi?

Let us now think for the betterment of India forgetting the past activity of Gandhi who had destroyed India by the movement of "Non-Violence". It is universally true that Unity is the strength of progress and prosperity.

Thus it is true; the USA is the Superpower due to the effort of unity of Black and white.

Let us "**SALUTE - Narendra Modi**" who has shown us the path of progress. Now INDIANS are hoping for a better future.

Q.No. 35 - Because the Prime Minister of the UK, Rishi Sunak will become the MOST Powerful Hindu Leader in the World! Can BJP, RSS & all ModiBhakts do anything to STOP their TALLEST Leader Narendra Modi being overtaken by Rishi Sunak in IMPORTANCE among Hindus at Global Level?

Gandhi became a great person of India through the policy of falsehood of "Non-Violence" killing millions of Indians and displacing the millions by the division of India, Modi became popular after the Godra incident and Gujarat Rioting but not a great humanitarian like Abraham Lincoln, who had united the USA. But Modi brought the peace in Gujarat through Modi riot instead of Gandhi's "NON VIOLENCE" bringing Calcutta Riot in the name CALCUTTA KILLING, 16th August. Thus violence is required sometimes to regulate administration. The Atom Bomb was necessary to stop World War.

Politics of India is guided by few people who are cunning and power mongers.

Bengal was important during the independence movement where the prominent leader Gandhi succeeded to divide Bengal. Now again after 70 years, the Election of Bengal became an important election- why? Is it for the reunion of Bengal?

Union or Reunion is a natural issue. The objective of the nation is to live in peace and prosperity. The UK united the Islands and made economic prosperity that is why the UK is a great country even though it is a small country with respect to area and population. Thus for the prosperity of Bengal the Bengalis need unity of all people irrespective of religion. The union of INDIA, PAKISTAN and BANGLADESH is a necessity to bring prosperity to united British INDIA.

Q.No. 36 - What is the connection of Subhas Chandra Bose with Jagadish Chandra Bose, Satyendra nath Bose and Amar Bose?

Subash Chandra Bose was no other than Netaji, who thought for India to be liberated by Azaid-Hind-Fauz and make it a country of humanity, a country of Super-power. Sir Jagadish Chandra Bose was a scientist. Again

Satyendranath Bose was a student of Jagadish Chandra Bose, he worked with Sir Albert Einstein. But all kinds of activity went down under Gandhi's falsehood of "NON-VIOLENCE" in the name of the activity of INDEPENDENT MOVEMENT OF INDIA.

Q.No. 37 - What has been done by the WB government to honour Subhas Chandra Bose in the last 15 years?

Nothing but fighting for Chair. Dr. S P Mukherjee became a fool in the name of "Hindu-Bengal". He finally got nothing but the death penalty inside the jail of Kashmir. Bengal was destroyed by Gandhi first by "Non-Violence "and then by division. Poverty prevailed everywhere in Bengal. CPM became a champion Party but brought nothing but poverty because Bengal Industry brought by British administration was demolished under Gandhi's movement of "NON_VIOLENCE". The Congress or any other Government could not find time to think of any prize for Subhas Chandra Bose, (Netaji).

Q.No. 38 - Owaisi equates attack on himself with attack on Mahatma Gandhi. What's your reaction?

Owaisi attacked Gandhi- nothing wrong although I don't know what he said. But the fact is that Gandhi, a self-centered person destroyed beautiful India by division for his name and fame making Nehru the PM instead of the fittest person Jinnah. Gandhi was the worst creature of the Universe because he thought for himself to make name and fame at the cost of the country.

Q.No. 39 - Which God is known as the destroyer of the universe according to Hindu mythology?

"The Great Gandhi of India." He not only destroyed India by division but even destroyed humanity befooling the members of the UN through the indiscipline of "non-violence" and made himself a **man of peace** through the falsehood speech of Indian PM NEHRU. The object of PEACE was highlighted through the activity of "NON-VIOLENCE" and the object of killing millions through "NON-VIOLENCE" under rioting and under "DIVISION" kept under carpet. B**engal was a place of humanity but it turned Islam for power politics which originated in the atmosphere of CALCUTTA KILLING on every day of 16**th **AUGUST of 1946 due to "NON-VIOLENCE" activity of Gandhi at CALCUTTA.**

Q.No. 40 - Why did the United Bengal state fail to form?

It was because (i) Gandhi wanted to kick out Jinnah from India (ii) Gandhi wanted to destroy Bengal so that leaders like Subash Bose was not born in Bengal (iii) Nehru, Petal Kripanali and Rajendra Prasad wanted a smaller Bengal so that PM never be from Bengal.

Q.No. 41 - Where do we stand after 75 years of Independence?

To know the real facts, we must know the earlier history, where Hindu Bengalis acted as foolish Bengalis and many Indian leaders acted for self-image and personal pleasure of sexual life. Let us start with Bengal. Bengal was divided by few leaders. Suhrawardy, the then PM of Bengal misguided under the command of Jinnah, brought out rioting in Calcutta but very soon realized the mistake and wanted to form "A Sovereign United Bengal" along with Satis Bose, the brother of Subhas Boser (Netaji). But Shyamas Prasad Mukherjeewas misguided by other Northern Indian leaders and encouraged to form "HINDU HOME LAND ".

But in the end no "HINDU HOME LAND " was formed and in the end Mukherjee was sacked from the Ministry and finally he was kept in JAIL in Kashmir and allowed him to die in JAIL. This was the intelligence activity of Bengal leader Mukherjee.

Politics of India is guided by few people who were better cunning as well as better power mongers than Mukherjee for which he has one taken in the Ministry, but in right time he has been sacked from the Ministry and finally kept in the jail of KASHMIR when his cry for "HINDU HOME LAND" had never heard of. The foolish Bengal Leader Mr. Mukherjee had no other alternative but to die inside the jail of Kashmir.

Jawaharlal Nehru and Indira Gandhi did not agree to even reasonable demands of Hindus during their rule. Still Hindus were electing them to power with a high majority. Why?

It was because Hindus were fools, and dark in religion because of cowardness. They never learn how to live together, because they are selfish, they like to love themselves. They were greedy. They sacrificed their 12-year-old girl to 70-year-old Brahmins to marry, and burn-in the funeral along with her alive. It was the sacrifice to Gods in heaven on their part. It was because they were keeping their space in heaven which is required for them after their death. It was great for them, the intelligent Bengalis were living with those beliefs.

Nehru became **Interested in Politics** as he failed in the Practice of Law, although the place of Practice of Law was a center long before had been established by his FATHER Motilal Nehru.

Q.No. 42 - What was the relation of Jawaharlala Nehru and Gandhi ji?

Gandhi knew he could not do anything on his own, he required Nehru as he was foolish to some extent and a son of a renowned person the Great Advocate Motilal Nehru.

Nehru was the son of a rich man. Although he was very poor in the practice of law still he claims to be one of the great personalities of India because of his Father's money and money power. Getting Gandhi well, he began to think about getting the PM post of India once after the liberation of India. Thus people could see Gandhi made Nehru the PM instead of elected candidate Petal. Nehru in the end made Gandhi the "FATHER OF THE NATION" and also a man of peace in the UN.

What was the objective of these political leaders, to do good to the public or to increase their own power of chair? Afterwards it became clear that the objective was how to become the PM of India (Nehru) and how to become the FATHER of the Nation (Gandhi).

Q.No. 43 - What is this whole process of the creation of Pakistan ?

If you want a frank answer to this question, in view of a white American it can be viewed as an Indian-Civil-War which is still ongoing and now has an added nuclear dimension to it.

To a large extent Gandhi was responsible for this unhappy state of affairs in the Indian subcontinent, because he did not do enough to prevent it or was hidebound by his rigid convictions to think outside the box - of different ways to prevent it.

Let us explain it better:

Gandhi and Nehru (his political successor and protege) had neither the political acumen to see into the future nor the will to implement a grand vision for India and their non-violent Puritanism was actually a very inhibiting factor in nation-building in 1947.

Patel was much more astute and savvy in these matters and had a very good grasp of Real politics.

Honestly speaking, according to a white American who has traveled to both India and Pakistan and knows first hand the situation on the ground, who had explained it better in the following impartial manner.

If the Muslims were/are a sizable minority in any country, even in the USA, UK, Australia or Russia for that matter, the process of Pakistanization - or -

"Islamist-Supremacist-Secessionist agitation accompanied by violent struggle and supported by frequent acts of terror against a host nation, for the establishment of a separate Islamic country in a host nation" is very much a possibility.

EU may face this situation in the next few years where burgeoning Muslim populations in the EU may start attacking and terrorizing Europeans to give them a separate Islamic State in Southern Europe (Spain)

So this process of Pakistanization which was successful in the case of India in the year 1947, is not just restricted to that unfortunate country alone.

It can even happen in China if the population of Uighurs reaches 33% of the Chinese population or Australia or South Africa if Muslims population in these countries reaches 33% of the total population.

For the record it is currently happening in Nigeria where Boko Haram is terrorizing non-Muslim Nigerians on a daily basis and also in Indian Kashmir (where Kashmiri Pandits have been chased out of their homeland) by Islamist fanatics sponsored by Pakistan.

Now let us draw some parallels to the US civil war where Americans had to face a similar nation-fracturing phase..in their history.

Let us go over the US-Civil war history in the US, there was no third party like the British involved. The Americans were the captains of their own destiny with no power like the British overseeing the civil war.

Another historic fact one needs to consider is that the British were preoccupied with and exhausted after the Sepoy rebellion in India which broke out in 1857, and had just concluded a few years before the outbreak of the American Civil War.

This prevented the British from siding with the Southern-Secessionist-Slave states against the Northern Unionist-Free States in the US Civil War of 1861-65.

Lincoln who was the president at that time, emphatically declared in his famous: Lincoln's House Divided Speech:

A house divided against itself cannot stand. He said I believe this government cannot endure, permanently, half slave and half free. I do not expect the Union to be dissolved.

(Now that is a great speech which all Indian politicians should read to get into their mindset and internalize it.)

Jefferson Davis - who was the equivalent of a Jinnah in the US, and President of the Southern Secessionist States, decided to split the US into two countries in 1861 and attacked the Northern states who were in favor of the Union and abolition of Slavery all over the US.

Three years after making his speech, Lincoln was not afraid of waging a brutal war to preserve the Union, even if it meant the use of maximum force, strategy and violence which resulted in the deaths of tens of thousands of fellow Americans who fought bitterly for the Secessionist Southern states which supported slavery.

In the case of the US, the Unionists had a crushing victory over the secessionists in 1865 and the Union of the United States was preserved and this allowed the Americans to become the world power that is visible today.

Unfortunately, for India, and the Indian people, INDIAN had a leader whose rigid convictions prevented him from indulging in a war to prevent the partition of India, nor did the person whom he appointed as his political successor -Nehru who was a weakling, a Pacifist and an active proponent of "non-violence" himself, have the stomach for a quick war which if he had mobilized the Indian people and launched in 1951, would have settled the matter in 1954 itself.

This was around the same time The People's Republic of China which also came into being under Mao in 1949, (two years after India gained independence) quickly used their People's Liberation Army to annex Tibet - which was larger or almost equal in area to Pakistan.

Moreover, Pakistan was British Premier Winston Churchill's pet idea and was fully supported by first the British and later the American governments who at that time, had the idea of using Pakistan to contain Soviet expansionism South, towards the warmer waters of the Arabian Sea during the Cold war.

So anybody or any American, would feel that India and the Indian people were unfortunate on both counts in this nascent phase of their history. They were (and still are) saddled with the Partition OF BRITISH INDIA.

a) Bad or weak leaders like Gandhi who did not have the foresight to see the problems which would have stranded the subcontinent and still continue to do so today by allowing Pakistan to be formed and also acquire Nuclear weapons.

and

b) An inimical overseeing power: The British - who never had the interests of the Indian peoples in their hearts and minds and did everything in their power to support the partition of the Indian homeland and undermine the Indians.

The British hated the idea of having to give up possession of their prize colony India in 1947. India being the primary reason Britain had gained world power status in the 19th and early 20th Centuries and their parting gift or rather (kick) to the Indian people was this artificial-partition of the Indian homeland and the horrendous violence and unnecessary migrations which accompanied it.

Also Britain which was economically devastated after World War II wanted to use this inter-state rivalry between the two newly created states in the Indian subcontinent to sell weapons to both countries and benefit from this sales of weapons to boost their crippled economy.

Right now as an American politician, who is privy to US policy matters in this area, especially after the Bin-Laden episode, it can be said that a large majority of us Americans overwhelmingly prefer that Pakistan is dissolved as soon as possible and merged back into India after a swift bloody war which kills off all or 95% of the Islamic fundamentalists in the Indian subcontinent.

If after this final Union of India is accomplished, - which is good for India, Pakistan and Bangladesh and ultimately good for the world, the Indians can probably say:

The American civil war lasted 4 years from 1861-1965, ours unfortunately lasted 4 score years from 1947-2024 or more.

Q.No. 44 - Why did Gandhi heavily favor Muslims over Hindus?

Gandhi favored Muslims over Hindus because:

He wanted both Hindus and Muslims to join together to fight against the British. So by pleasing Muslims, he felt that they would join Hindus to overthrow colonial rule.

(But he didn't realize that at the time of independence, Muslims would ask for a separate nation)

He considered Muslims to be just like followers of any other religion.

Had Gandhi been alive today and watched the formation of Islamic State, several countries with Islamic militant groups, many Muslims wanting Sharia law even in Western countries, Love Jihad etc; I doubt whether he would have favored Muslims over Hindus. He did not realize their actual nature back then and felt sympathetic towards them as they formed a minority in India. To him the British were a greater threat.

Q.No. 45(A) - What are the dark secrets of Mahatma Gandhi that are not exposed in public ?

Today, what is observed in any book of history in India finds Gandhiji to be hailed as "Father of the Nation", "Mahatma", "The person who is highly praised behind the independence of India".

Every book has discussed his principles of Ahimsa, Satyagraha and Non-Violence. But that's only one side of the coin. If someone wants to know the other side, it is certainly acceptable to consider him a selfish person and hate him beyond imagination. Here are some points to ponder upon.

1. Everybody praises him for the work which he did in South Africa for the slaves and is known to raise his voice against apartheid. But many of us don't know that in 1896, he gave a speech where he stated that the natives of RSA are **kaffirs** (A racist slur) whose main purpose is to hunt, buy some cattle and buy a wife with the sole purpose of living their lives in nakedness and indolence.

    This isn't the only instance. Once, he was sent to prison and was kept with the kaffirs in South Africa, he complained that the Indians are way above the black natives in RSA and their (Natives of RSA) lifestyle is that of an animal.

2. Gandhi proclaimed himself as a Hindu by faith, Gandhiji banned the song Vande Mataram which was not only worshiped by the Bengalis but also the national slogan against the uprising British in India. The song of Vande Mataram was discarded by Gandhi because of the inner fear of aggressive Jnnah. Because, it was Jinnah and his few Muslim followers who wanted a ban from this song and in

the Congress manifesto of 1940, they forbade their leaders to use this slogan while giving speeches.

Gandhi was PRO MUSLIMS AND ANTI HINDU because of inner fear of militant Muslims:

His love for muslims is well reflected by the fact that he demanded Hindu refugees to leave the mosque they occupied in Delhi and went for a fast till death for that. But he never uttered a single word when the newly formed Pakistan was brutally killing and torturing the Hindus there.

On 6th April 1947, he gave a speech where he said, **"If the Muslims are out there slicing through Hindu masses to wipe out the Hindu race, the Hindus should say nothing and peacefully accept death".**

He hated the great Hindu rulers especially Shivaji Maharaj. To please the Muslims, he banned the book named Shiv Bhavani which correctly depicted Islam's intolerance and fierce fundamentalism spread by it.

It is astonishing to hear his views what he said that **"If someone is out here raping your sister, all you should is fall on that person's feet and if he kills you, you should accept death".**

3. Gandhiji was a two faced snake. He actually maintained two papers- One in English and one in Gujarati. In English, he posed himself as an opposer of caste system, untouchability etc while in Gujarat he supported all those systems.

4. He was a big hypocrite. On one side, where he preached unity of Hindus and Muslims, on the other hand, he prevented his son from marrying a Muslim girl.

5. He publicly denounced parliamentary politics, lawyers whereas he was himself a lawyer, and argued that India should have its own parliament.

   What was Gandhi: A Saint or a Sinner?

6. Let's talk about the treatment he gave to his wife…… Kasturba Bai was suffering from pneumonia and a penicillin vaccine was the cure for that disease. But Gandhiji didn't allow her to take it because the medicine was against God and she died.

7. But, only a few weeks later, he was suffering from malaria and the doctor prescribed quinine, another alien drug, his faith in God vanished completely and allowed the doctors to administer the drug in order to survive. It was his Hypocrisy at its peak!!!

It is better not to mention his sex life. He actually slept naked with his grandniece Manu and his grandnephew's wife Abha together.

Gandhiji was not a saint at all. He doesn't deserve to be called " Father of the Nation". He doesn't deserve to have his image on the currency notes. He was the reason that India had to wait so long for its independence. His views were so pathetic, corrupt that one would really want to erase all his history from India.

As an Author I salute all the people who gave their lives for India. Bhagat Singh, Rani Laxmi Bai, Sardar Patel, Netaji Subhash Chandra Bose and his Azad Hind Fauj and many more. Had Netaji taken the charge, India would have been a much better nation today. But, Gandhiji didn't want him in the INC because he knew that Netaji was going to expose him completely.

Q.No. 45(B) - How does it feel to be labelled as an 'Illegal Bangladeshi' for an Indian Bengali Muslim?

Bengal was a place of humanity but it turned Islam for power politics.

Gandhi made all the Muslims of Bengal enemy by the religious movement "Non-Violence"and created violence, now in Assam as the picture shows all

these ordinary Muslims citizens are designed as Bangladeshi and going to be enemy, will it be good for Hindus of India? If these people belong to India, why are they compelled to come out with a certificate in hand with a crying voice. Their safety is the pride of every Indian. Their suffering is the sufferings of every Indian.

Q.No. 46(A) - What is it like to be an Indian Bengali Muslim? An Indian Bengali Muslim from here in WB.

The answer to this question depends on the respective socio-economic condition of Bengali Muslims in India.

As for a person who is a single child of working, educated parents, was among top 50 students in WB state board exams and has attended one of the most prestigious higher education institutions in India through a national competitive examination as a general category student. They were 3 Bengali Muslim students in a total student strength of 900 in that institution selected across India.

Their folks were wealthy 'Ashraf' zamindars (upper-class and caste feudal landlords) in Rarh Bengal (western part of West Bengal), the oldest ancestor (with Muslim name) that They have records of survived in 1700 AD and were proficient in Farsi which was the court language of

Bengal at that time, one he is from 15ᵗʰ generation in the same family. In the 1800s his ancestors were involved in silk farming, leather tannery as well as indigo cultivation along with East India company officials and probably at that time they expanded the Zamindari by buying lands. Over the years his forefathers mismanaged vast inherited wealth and subsequent generations became relatively less wealthy living off inheritance, but the snobbishness towards work and 'Babugiri' continued as usual. They had plenty of graduates and one ICS officer in the family and some relatives worked with Bengal Congress and with the Communist Party in the pre-partition Era. Finally they lost their last inherited land holdings in 1977 land reforms, they could not transform their inherited wealth into successful private business like some of the other contemporary Bengali Hindu wealthy families with whom they had business relations. For eg. His great grandmother was a patron of PC Chandra who founded the house of PC Chandra Jewellers in Kolkata and Jewellery as per her specification were sent from their workshop in Kolkata to their ancestral home for all family occasions on credit.

Currently he would classify themselves as middle class with similar lifestyle, goals and ambition like other middle-class Bengali Hindus living in Kolkata surviving on monthly salary from stable jobs with utmost importance given to education of children. Almost all their relatives are masters - degree holders and work in Govt jobs, primarily in bureaucracy, judiciary and academics, a lot of them practise medicine and law as well. Very few work in the private sector and private sector jobs and business in general is looked at with contempt. He has grown up in a town with 60% Muslims in Rarh Bengal with absolute communal harmony, in his college under friend circle was 100% Hindu, faced some religious prejudiced comments sometimes (only in Kolkata, never in his hometown) but never faced any religious discrimination firsthand within WB, their Kolkata home is in 99% Bengali Hindu majority housing society and they have never felt any kind of unease, have participated in Saraswati Puja and Eid Milads in school (our school used to organize both) and Durga puja in their Kolkata housing society. In fact as far as he remembered they have always avoided living with non-Bengali, Urdu - speaking Muslims who constitute 90% of all Muslims living in Kolkata and Bengali Muslims find it extremely difficult to mingle with them as their cultural practices and customs vary a lot. Normally they consider them very conservative and they consider them less observant /deviant (some even consider them crypto-Hindus) who wear Sarees /bindis, women do not follow Purdah and eat rice & fish.

There is much more commonality among middle-class Bengali Hindus and middle-class Bengali Muslims than the commonality among Bengali Hindus and non-Bengali Hindus or Bengali Muslims and non-Bengali Muslims. In fact one could see much more inter-religious marriages taking place among Bengali Hindus and Bengali Muslims than among Bengali Muslims and non-Bengali Muslims.

But still his family is an outlier, overall Bengali Muslims in WB are very poor, not well educated and politically not well organized (basically pawns) as they are spread across rural areas. The Bengali Muslim middle-class in WB was a very tiny section unlike Bengali Hindus till the 1970s.

Most of the middle-class Bengali Muslims moved to East Bengal after 1971 for better fortunes (including a small section of their relatives) and the people who remained were either wealthy (micro - minority) or dirt poor. Nowadays all Bengali Muslims neo middle-class have emerged in WB who are aspirational and suffer from the same unemployment and other problems like other

Bengali Hindu OBCs and SCs. A section of non-Ashraf Bengali Muslims have also started business enterprises and found success but access to credit and bank loans remains an issue.

But as far as the poorer vast majority of Bengali Muslims are concerned they are involved in farming (more than 40% of WB farmers), fishing, weaving and other kind of blue collar jobs and mostly recent-converts from very backward Hindu communities involved in similar profession which have been the same for centuries. Bengali Muslims as a community is 25% of total population of West Bengal but politically vastly under represented as Muslim political leaders in leading political parties of WB come from tiny Urdu - speaking Muslim community (2% of WB population) born and brought up in cities like Kolkata, Asansol etc and they are not true representative of the interests and requirements of Bengali Muslim community in WB, yet they set the political agenda harming interests of Bengali Muslims, this is actually more prominent in TMC administration than during Left front rule. Besides, very few people are aware of a indigenous large Bengali Muslim community outside West Bengal.

What he had mentioned here is for only Bengali Muslims of West Bengal, India not for Bengali Muslims in Jharkhand, Eastern Bihar, Assam, Manipur and Tripura.

Q.No. 46(B) - How do Bangladeshis feel about their citizens illegally migrating to India?..

India is a tourist and medical destination for Bangladeshis but settling in India for livelihood is extremely rare. I don't deny that there are Bangladeshis in India but the number is disputed.

Indian and Bangladeshi economic conditions are not very different. India has a stronger economy but Bangladesh being a much smaller country isn't far behind. The living standard is comparatively better than many Indian states.

Bangladeshis who go abroad for work go to the Middle East (Unskilled & less educated folks mainly) and USA, UK, Japan, Australia (semi-skilled & highly skilled folks). India is not a work destination for Bangladeshis.

Bangladeshis view India as a natural ally and development partner. Why ruin such a relationship by bringing up such a controversial issue? Those who went to India in 1971 to escape from Pak army and Bengali Razakars (those locals who helped Pak army) returned back post independence of Bangladesh but only some thousands remained in India and never returned. These people have every right to live in India because they were living in India when Bangladesh was not created. So technically they were not Bangladeshis.

Bangladesh is a part of India in a broader sense since the region was called East Bengal, a province of India until 1947. Culturally all Bangladeshis are Indians. We look the same, talk similar and behave similarly.

This issue of immigrants will always be there since there is no way to prove or disprove it. There is no natural barrier between the two nations. So it's better to ignore this issue.

Q.No. 47 - What actually got independence for India - Congress or Freedom Fighters or Mahatma Gandhi or something else?

The British quit their colonies for two reasons - the Colonies became dry and then the changed world post WWII gave rise to "Nationalist" sentiments everywhere.

Why did the British quit India? The answer might be here: John Maynard Keynes warned that the British debt had risen to 3000 million Pounds. (The Untold Story of India's Partition: Narendra Singh Sarila)

There are multiple factors working together to make the British leave India **on their own terms -**

1. Mounting pressure from the Independence movement from within India was a factor but **continued loyalty of the armed forces was a serious question.** The British officers had the prospect of a mutiny on their hands. Post WW2, freshly demobilized soldiers had no job, no money, nothing to occupy their minds, no livelihood but plenty of capability to plan, organize and execute rebellion. As such, such ex-soldiers who returned to their native villages took active part in partition violence. The minor mutiny of naval officers at Bombay was an example.

2. Changed the international political scene after WWII.

3. **Financial difficulties in Britain**. The country needed intensive effort to recoup after the War. **John Maynard Keynes,** the economist, warned the Labour government soon after they assumed power that the British debt had risen to 3000 million Pounds. In 1947, it was a very huge amount!

4. **The cost of maintaining colonies**. Keynes also warned that out of the above number, **2000 million pounds** was due to the cost of policing & administering the Empire.

Cynical it may sound, the British had milked the cow dry and there was nothing more coming out of the colonies' udder.

6. Pressure from the USA. Their **Atlantic Charter** demanded de-colonization.

7. Churchill falling out of favor post WWII. Even when Churchill was in power, Attlee was strongly in favor of quitting India.

According to Attlee, the factors #3 and #4 weighed heavily in the decision to quit India and other colonies.

[Clement Attlee had better sense]

In spite of the above factors, **Churchill was dead against quitting India**. Prime Minister Attlee needed his support for passing the India Independence Bill and he sent Mountbatten to his home to convince. Churchill extracted a personal promise from Mountbatten to the effect that all the princely states of India would be given freedom to remain independent (of the two new countries). This meant, **Churchill wanted Balkanization of India** (and Pakistan too, to some extent).

After passing of the Bill, Churchill realized that he was misled by Mountbatten and refused to even greet him.

Q.No. 48 - Originally Answered by few Indians : What would have happened to the Indian independence movement without Gandhi?

There was an ongoing freedom struggle (1885 to 1915) even before Gandhi joined it. There were leaders like Tilak & Gokhale. So had Gandhi not come, still the Indian freedom struggle would have continued.

In absence of Gandhi, the struggle would have been a bit more violent because Gandhi was a pacifist and did not allow violence. So more Indians would have martyred at the altar of freedom. It is quite probable that Gandhi's place would have been taken by Subhash Chandra Bose because Bose became the President of Congress in 1938 against Gandhi's wishes and defeating the man Gandhi had nominated. Bose was more aggressive and approved of violent means also for achieving freedom - if called for.

India would have gained freedom after the end of World War-2 even if Gandhi was not there, just like other countries which did not have a Gandhi - like Burma &

Sri Lanka. The British did not leave India because of the August 1942 'Quit India' movement launched by Gandhi / Congress and calls given by them to 'Do or Die'. Gandhi launched this movement with all the strength he had and this time he was okay if as result of his call some Indians adopted violence.

The British suppressed the Quit India Movement just as any war-time Govt would do and it petered out. By May 1944 even Gandhi was released from Jail as the Quit India Movement had died down.

The British decided to withdraw from India and grant independence because

[i] Britain was weakened beyond all limits in the War with Germany. London had been ruined by Hitler's bombing, many young Englishmen had dies in the war and the remaining wanted to go home rather than serve in India & other colonies, economy in Great Britain was shattered, it owed huge financial debt to Govt of India;

[ii] Britain was no more sure of support of loyal British Indian Army which was its final strength. War in Burma with Azad Hind Fauz had proved that Indian

Sepoys would turn against British rulers in India given proper leadership.

So had Gandhi not been there, the British would have still left India after World War-2.

The next question is what could be other consequences of the absence of Gandhi? According to general view, Subhash was more accepted as a leader by Muslims than Gandhi. Azad Hind Fauz had many Muslims. During tenure as CEO of Calcutta Municipal Corporation (1924), Subhash was able to carry the Muslims better. (It is there in the book 'His Majesty's Opponent' by Sugata Bose).

India's freedom was a foregone conclusion and the British were eager to leave & go. It got delayed till 15th Aug 1947 only because the Congress and Muslim League could not agree on a power-sharing formula in the free India's Govt.

Since Subhash would have been the leader in absence of Gandhi and since Muslims had greater trust on him, and since he was more progressive - it is likely that partition could have been avoided and that India would have got freedom earlier than 15th Aug 1947.

Well this is speculative history!!

Let us see : - [Content of History in disguise]:

It is right or wrong no matter what. There are so many misconceptions about our history because of false information spread by some politician who never picked up a book of history or read original works of the freedom fighters. Here is the speculation of a person, who had well read with original works of freedom fighters, read tons of history books, constitutional debates, philosophical works of Hinduism including Vedas, Buddhist philosophy among others. So it is here a balanced answer.

There were 4 major stages in freedom struggle:

1. **Struggle under Moderates:** Moderates included people like WC Banerjee, Dadabhai Naoroji and Gokhale. They were one of the first people who demanded self rule. But their methods of protest were not very extreme. They published their views through newspapers, journals and other print media or used methods like petitions and prayers to the British govt. They never demanded complete independence and were happy with just self rule.

2. **Struggle under Extremists:** The extremists include Lal, Bal, Pal among others. They used methods like agitations and strikes. They propounded the ideas of swaraj and swadeshi. They were not afraid of the British. They founded nationalist colleges

and supported nationalist industries. The Vande mataram and National Anthem were written during this stage.

3. **Struggle under revolutionaries:** Revolutionaries included surya sen, Bhagat Singh, Sukhdev among others. They formed secret societies and attacked British officials on a case by case basis. The HRA was formed which was later renamed to HSRA. The revolutionaries came to action during the 1890s (at the same time when extremists became active). Bhagat Singh and comrades in their later stages understood that murdering a few officers is not creating a desired effect. The people at large are unaware of their goals and ideology. Therefore, he decided to throw bombs in an empty assembly hall and get arrested.

4. **Struggle under Gandhi:** BEFORE THE ARRIVAL of Gandhi, the freedom movement was limited to the Urban centres and major towns. There was no change in the life of villagers and more than 90% of the Indians lived in villages. Gandhi knew that to get freedom, masses will have to get involved. He developed the strategy of mass movements and brought masses into the struggle for freedom. In

the NCM of the 1920s, the whole nation was swept in. Even the revolutionaries like Bhagat Singh were brought into the fold of national movement.

IDEALISM OF GANDHI:

Gandhi was an idealist. That's where the problem began.

1. He believed that the Muslims and Hindus can live peacefully forever.

2. He believed that the mass movements should be very very peaceful.

3. He believed that the Indian villages can live self-sufficiently with small village based industries.

4. He believed that Pakistan would never hurt us.

He was an idealist. But idealism doesn't work all the time. This had its own positives and negatives.

Q.No. 49 - Is Mahatma Gandhi really responsible for India's freedom?

Role of Mahatma Gandhi in India's freedom was "minimal". His role in bringing people together and organizing a mass movement cannot be discounted but in terms of forcing the British out, Subhash Chandra Bose is the man. None other than British Prime minister of that time admitted it. Extracts of what he said:-

A statement given by PB Chakroborty, West Bengal's governor at the time of Attlee's visit in 1956.

When I was acting as Governor of West Bengal in 1956, Lord Clement Attlee who as the British Prime Minister in post-War years was responsible for India's freedom, visited India and stayed in Raj Bhavan, Calcutta, for two days. 'The Quit India Movement of Gandhi practically died out long before 1947 and there was nothing in the Indian situation at that time, which made it necessary for the British to leave India in a hurry. Why then did they do so?'

In reply, Attlee cited several reasons, the most important of which were the INA activities of Netaji Subhas Chandra Bose, which weakened the very foundation of the British Empire in India, and the RIN mutiny which made the British realise that the Indian armed forces could no longer be trusted to prop up the British.

Role of Mahatma Gandhi in India's freedom was "minimal". His role in bringing people together and organizing a mass movement cannot be discounted but in terms of forcing the British out, Subhash Chandra Bose is the man. British PM

Attlee's visited CALCUTTA in 1956, and stayed in Raj Bhavan, Calcutta, for two days and put it straight to him like this: 'The Quit India Movement of Gandhi practically died out long before 1947 and there was nothing in the Indian situation at that time, which made it necessary for the British to leave India in a hurry. Why then did they do so?'

In reply, Attlee cited several reasons, the most important of which were the INA activities of Netaji Subhas Chandra Bose, which weakened the very foundation of the British Empire in India, and the RIN mutiny which made the British realise that the Indian armed forces could no longer be trusted to prop up the British.

Former Knowledge of Indian economics and Indian history at Chambers of Commerce (1966–2008)2y

Originally Answered: Why did Mahatma Gandhi agree to divide India?

There seems to be a misconception among some people that Mahatma Gandhi agreed to divide India. This is contrary to facts as he was very much opposed to this and in fact went on a fast and stayed away from celebrations on 15th August 1947, on the occasion of Independence.

The Partition of India had been demanded by the Indian Muslim League at the Lahore Resolution in 1940 by the demarcation of certain regions to constitute a homeland for the Muslims of India. The argument was put forward by Jinnah that Islam forbids Muslims to live under any form of non-Muslim governments and that democratically elected government in India would end up being non-Muslim due to overwhelming numbers of Hindus. Jinnah insisted for Pakistan and Gandhi finally agreed upon with going with force rather high lighted "NON-VIOLENCE:

Q.No. 50 - How do Bangladeshis feel about their citizens illegally migrating to India?

India is a tourist and medical destination for Bangladeshis but settling in India for livelihood is extremely rare. I don't deny that there are Bangladeshis in India but the number is disputed.

Indian and Bangladeshi economic conditions are not very different. India has a stronger economy but Bangladesh being a much smaller country isn't far behind. The living standard is comparatively better than many Indian states.

Bangladeshis who go abroad for work go to the Middle East (Unskilled & less educated folks mainly) and USA, UK, Japan, Australia (semi-skilled & highly skilled folks). India is not a work destination for Bangladeshis.

Bangladeshis view India as a natural ally and development partner. Why ruin such a relationship by bringing up such a controversial issue? Those who went to India in 1971 to escape from Pak army and Bengali Razakars (those locals who helped Pak army) returned back post independence of Bangladesh but only some thousands remained in India and never returned. These people have every right to live in India because they were living in India when Bangladesh was not created. So technically they were not Bangladeshis.

Bangladesh is a part of India in a broader sense since the region was called East Bengal, a province of India until 1947. Culturally all Bangladeshis are Indians. We look the same, talk similar and behave similarly.

This issue of immigrants will always be there since there is no way to prove or disprove it. There is no natural barrier between the two nations. So it's better to ignore this issue.

Q.No. 51 - What actually got independence for India - Congress or Freedom Fighters or Mahatma Gandhi or something else?

The British quit their colonies for two reasons - the Colonies became dry and then the changed world post WWII gave rise to "Nationalist" sentiments everywhere.

Why did the British quit India? The answer might be here: John Maynard Keynes warned that the British debt had risen to 3000 million Pounds.

There are multiple factors working together to make the British leave India **on their own terms -**

1. Mounting pressure from the Independence movement from within India was a factor but **continued loyalty of the armed forces was a serious question.** The British officers had the prospect of a mutiny on their hands. Post WW2, freshly demobilized soldiers had no job, no money, nothing to occupy their minds, no livelihood but plenty of capability to plan, organize and execute rebellion. As such, such ex-soldiers who returned to their native villages took active part in partition violence. The minor mutiny of naval officers at Bombay was an example.

2. Changed the international political scene after WWII.

3. **Financial difficulties in Britain**. The country needed intensive effort to recoup after the War. **John Maynard Keynes,** the economist, warned the Labour government soon after they assumed power that the British debt had risen to 3000 million Pounds. In 1947, it was a very huge amount!

4. **The cost of maintaining colonies**. Keynes also warned that out of the above number, **2000 million pounds** was due to the cost of policing & administering the Empire.

5. Cynical it may sound, the British had milked the cow dry and there was nothing more coming out of the colonies' udder.

6. Pressure from the USA. Their **Atlantic Charter** demanded de-colonization.

7. Churchill falling out of favor post WWII. Even when Churchill was in power, Attlee was strongly in favor of quitting India.

According to Attlee, the factors #3 and #4 weighed heavily in the decision to quit India and other colonies.

[Clement Attlee had better sense]

In spite of the above factors, **Churchill was dead against quitting India**. Prime Minister Attlee needed his support for passing the India Independence Bill and he sent Mountbatten to his home to convince. Churchill extracted a personal promise from Mountbatten to the effect that all the princely states of India would be given freedom to remain independent (of the two new countries). This meant, **Churchill wanted Balkanization of India** (and Pakistan too, to some extent).

After passing of the Bill, Churchill realized that he was misled by Mountbatten and refused to even greet him.

Q.No. 52 - GANDHI? WAS HE RESPONSIBLE FOR DELAYING FREEDOM?

It is under yes or no. He was the person who brought the masses from the corners of the country to the streets and disobeyed the British.

He was a master man manager and strategist. He called off NCM but didn't call off QIM despite knowing that people were employing huge violence. His moves were very calculated

His methods of protest were even more extreme than extremists. He broke the British laws. Started 3 major mass movements taking all the responsibility on his shoulders.

Moreover, the freedom struggle had more to do than just internal factors. The British after WW2 were Bankrupt. It was impossible for them to hold on to a big colony like India

The USSR after WW2 was supporting freedom of nations from colonial rule to increase the influence of communism throughout the world. So freedom of India was on cards.

BHAGAT SINGH AND GANDHI RTC CONTROVERSY:

The British had invited Gandhi on an equal footing to London to decide the future of India. Gandhi accepted the invitation because this was the 1st time when the British had decided to treat Indians as their equal and were willing to sit at the same table.

Gandhi had 2 choices: either to accept it and India may get self rule finally OR to not attend it (throwing away a significant offer that could prove to be a significant boost to India's freedom)

Finally Gandhi decided to go. The British didn't accept his demand. Bhagat Singh was hanged. CDM 2 was launched

We can't predict the future. Things are not as simple as they are portrayed.

GANDHI AND HIS ROLE IN PARTITION:

He was against the partition. The cabinet mission meetings, Cripps mission, Desai Liaqat talks, Rajaji formula- everything failed because Gandhi and co. were against partition.

In the end, Jinnah gave the call for direct action day. Thousands of people died in a day and whole India was in the flames of Communal violence.

Finally to stop the bloodshed Gandhi agreed to partition.

He speeded up the freedom movement. On the other note, there are many people in India especially from religious groups like Hindu Mahasabha, Muslim groups, RSS etc. that portray Gandhi in bad light.

Many of these organizations didn't even want India to get independent.

WAS HE RESPONSIBLE FOR DELAYING FREEDOM?

It is in between yes or no. He was the person who brought the masses from the corners of the country to the streets and disobeyed the British.

The movement proceeded slowly with the atmosphere of "NON-VIOLENCE". The British after WW2 were Bankrupt. It was impossible for them to hold on to a big colony like India

The USSR after WW2 was supporting freedom of nations from colonial rule to increase the influence of communism throughout the world. So freedom of India was on cards.

BHAGAT SINGH AND GANDHI RTC CONTROVERSY:

The British had invited Gandhi on an equal footing to London to decide the future of India. Gandhi accepted the invitation because this was the 1st time when the British had decided to treat Indians as their equal and were willing to sit at the same table.

Gandhi had 2 choices: either to accept it and India may get self rule finally OR to not attend it.

He decided to go. The British didn't accept his demand. Bhagat Singh was hanged.

GANDHI AND HIS ROLE IN PARTITION:

He was against the partition. The cabinet mission meetings, Cripps mission, Desai Liaqat talks, Rajaji formula- everything failed because Gandhi and co. were against partition.

In the end, Jinnah gave the call for direct action day. Thousands of people died in a day and whole India was in the flames of Communal violence.

To stop bloodshed Gandhi finally agreed to partition.

On the other note, there are many people in India especially from religious groups like Hindu Mahasabha, Muslim groups, RSS etc. that portray Gandhi in bad light.

Many of these organizations didn't even want India to get independent.

Q.No. 53 - How different would the Indian freedom struggle have been without Mahatma Gandhi?

We could have attained independence some 10–15 years earlier without facing Partition had Gandhi been absent on the Indian scene.

Congress was a party founded by the British mainly in 1885 with the objective of preventing Indians from going into direct open war against them (100 crore of Indians from undivided India vs 75000 British feringhees).

In 1857 the British had burnt their fingers as Indian revolutionaries won territories from Delhi to Bengal to Gwalior and literally threw out the British from there for a brief time, which the British never forgot and often worked to avoid open confrontation with the Indians. The British were for the same reason also scared of Netaji Bose's Azad Hind Fouz and the Naval Mutiny of 1946 as they knew they didn't stand any chance to withstand the onslaught. The British left India but caused damage in the form of Partition and by ensuring that a reportee Congress party stays in power to report to them after they had left.

The Congress also after Gandhi's arrival on the scene took up the agenda of Muslim appeasement which played a catalyst in Partition due to appeasement of Muslim demands.

Muslims initiated aggression and killed Hindus in the Noakhali riots but when Hindus retaliated the Congress leaders and Gandhi asked the Hindus to kill them first before harming the Muslims.

Gandhi takes a Rs 100 pension from the British per month to ensure that Indians don't get violent.

Here is a book everyone should read and **Jump to ratings and reviews**:

Want to read [2nd EDITION]

Kindle $3.99

The Dark Side of Gandhi of Hari Pada Roychoudhury:

It is a learning lesson for all political leaders of the World to see and learn how a villainous person can make fool the countrymen having a Dress of half naked FAKIR (in the words of Winston Churchill) with his ethics of "Non-Violence" bringing division, destruction, slaughter in millions and then the mankind with "Non-Violence" when United Nations Secretary commented the person is a man of peace of mankind.

232 pages, Kindle Edition

Published April 29, 2019, Page-102

Q.No. 54 - Had the Indian political situation been different if Mahatma Gandhi was to stay alive for few more years post independence? How?

Answered: Hypothetically speaking, would the Indian political situation have been very different, if Mr. Gandhi got to live a few more years post Independence? How?

Things would have been much worse. Gandhi was soft on Pakistan. He opposed the Government of India when it stopped the payment of Rs 55 crores as partition dues to Pakistan, in light of their 1948 invasion of Kashmir.

Gandhi went on a fast till death to pressure the Government of India in releasing the funds to Pakistan and succeeded. This of course didn't please the Army and Sardar Patel, who was tasked with the unification of princely states with the Dominion of India.

Gandhi was a staunch advocate of non-violence and with his pressure tactics, India would not have the ability to take armed action against the Nizam of Hyderabad, the Nawab of Junagarh, or the Portuguese in Goa.

Gandhi's idea of non-violence was to show your other cheek when someone slapped you. This idea persisted till the 1962 war. But after the defeat by China, India realized that to preach non-violence, it must be strong so that no one dared to slap even once.

This is why India has a nuclear triad now. The threats from our enemies cannot be ignored and we must not show them the other cheek if they slap us. Weakness is the greatest provocation of violence, and India's non-violence policy did more harm than good.

Q.No. 55 - If Sardar Vallabhai Patel comes back to life in today's India, what would be his reaction?

For obvious reasons, He would be sad as well as furious. He will notice how self-greed and selfish motives have taken over politics today. No politician is either motivated or interested in thinking about the nation. Every one eye's politics as a business for profits. And on top of that, his name is being used repeatedly and in comparison to Nehru and Gandhi for political gains. His anger is justified.

Back in his days, a politician was a leader of the masses and humble by nature. All they used to think of was 'Swaraj' and freedom from foreign people. They used to stay in jails or face lathi charge but never used to retaliate due to the principles of 'ahimsa' taught by the father of the nation. Leaders left their lucrative jobs, families, and society to fight the freedom war. It was a totally different act altogether. And that still reflects today as people remember them for their good deeds and sacrifices.

What's happening today is really pathetic. And it is going on even at the grass root level of the country. Even at the village level, only an influential and wealthy goon can fight the local election. The deserving candidates are made silent by some way or the other. The voice of the local people is bought with money or wine, in lieu of votes.

I hope you got the answer to your question! Apologize for harsh words, if any.

Q.No. 56 - What would Mahatma Gandhi think of after seeing the current state of India?

I think he would be shocked to see how the country, which he once helped liberate from the clutches of western imperialism, has fallen into the hands of western consumerism.

Nature produces enough to meet the needs of all the people, but not enough to satisfy the greed of any man. -Mahatma Gandhi

On one hand, he would be glad that India has managed to lift millions of people out of abject poverty. But on the other hand, he would be aghast seeing the mindless material consumption and the western way of life that is prevalent in some sections of society.

He thought that the western economic system, i.e. capitalism, was both unsustainable and devastating to the environment and the human spirit. Gandhi was a simple man and led a simple life. He wanted the country to have economic self-sufficiency without an emphasis on material pursuits or compromising human development.

Q.No. 57 - What is the Summary Discussion about Gandhi] ?

A Summary Discussion about Gandhi with respect to the earlier question which was as follows:

What are the dark secrets of Mahatma Gandhi that are not exposed in public ?

In CONCLUSION in India everywhere in India or outside Gandhi is regarded highly as a super human being and considered in the UN as a man of peace of the UNIVERSE.

In India everywhere Gandhiji is hailed as "Father of the Nation", and "Mahatma".

But with respect to the question of -What are the dark secrets of Mahatma Gandhi that are not exposed in public can be pointed in a nutshell.

"The person who is highly praised behind the independence of India was not so. Ahimsa, and Non-Violence is highly praised in the regions of India. Nobody thought of anything bad about INDIA and still regarded him a SAINT. This was the one sided belief about Gandhi.

But the other side is rarely discussed or thought over by any Indians. It is rarely acceptable to someone that he was the most selfish person and hated people beyond imagination. Here are some points to be highlighted that would satisfy every individual that existed everywhere in the UNIVERSE that he was the worst creature of the UNIVERSE.

[[The following few facts highlighted earlier might be looked into.]]

1. Everybody praises him for the work which he did in South Africa for the slaves and is known to raise his voice against apartheid. But many of us don't know that in 1896, he gave a speech where he stated that the natives of RSA are **kaffirs** (A racist slur) whose

main purpose is to hunt, buy some cattle and buy a wife with the sole purpose of living their lives in nakedness and indolence.

This isn't the only instance. Once, he was sent to prison and was kept with the kaffirs in South Africa. Hecomplained that lifestyle Africans are like that of an animal.

2. Gandhi proclaimed himself as a Hindu by faith, Gandhiji banned the song Vande Mataram which was not only worshiped by the Bengalis but also regarded as the national slogan against the uprising of the British in India. The song of Vande Mataram was discarded by Gandhi because of the inner fear of militant Muslims and aggressive Jnnah. Because, it was Jinnah and his few Muslim followers who wanted a ban from this song and in the Congress manifesto of 1940, they forbade their leaders to use this slogan while giving speeches.

3. **Gandhi was PRO MUSLIMS AND ANTI HINDU because of inner fear of militant Muslims:**

His love for Muslims is well reflected by the fact that he demanded Hindu refugees to leave the mosque they occupied in Delhi and went for a fast till death for that. But he never uttered a single word when the newly formed Pakistan was brutally killing and torturing the Hindus there.

4. On the 6th April 1947, he gave a speech where he said, " **If the Muslims are out there slicing through Hindu masses to wipe out the Hindu race, the Hindus should say nothing and peacefully accept death".**

He hated the great Hindu rulers especially Shivaji Maharaj.

It is astonishing to hear his views what he said that **"If someone is out here raping your sister, all you should is fall on that person's feet and if he kills you, you should accept death".**

5. He was a big hypocrite. On one side, where he preached unity of Hindus and Muslims, on the other hand, he prevented his son from marrying a Muslim girl.

6. He publicly denounced parliamentary politics, lawyers whereas he was himself a lawyer, and argued that India should have its own parliament.

What was Gandhi: A Saint or a Sinner?

Let's talk about the treatment he gave to his wife......
Kasturba Bai was suffering from pneumonia and a

penicillin vaccine was the cure for that disease. But Gandhiji didn't allow her to take it because the medicine was against God and she died.

But, only a few weeks later, he was suffering from malaria and the doctor prescribed quinine, another alien drug, his faith in God vanished completely and allowed the doctors to administer the drug in order to survive. It was his Hypocrisy at its peak!!!

It is better not to mention his sex life.He actually slept naked with his grandniece Manu and his grandnephew's wife Abha together.

Gandhiji was not a SAINT at all. He doesn't deserve to be called " Father of the Nation". He doesn't deserve to have his image on the currency notes. He was the reason that India had to wait so long for its independence. His views were so pathetic, corrupt that one would really want to erase all his history from India.

As an Author I salute all the people who gave their lives for India. Bhagat Singh, Rani Laxmi Bai, Sardar Patel, Netaji Subhash Chandra Bose and his Azad Hind Fauj and many more. Had Netaji taken the charge, India would have been a much better nation today. But, Gandhiji didn't want him in the INC because he knew that Netaji was going to expose him completely.

[In the end a tribute to PM Modiji by a publication of the NET].

An Indian never wants to hurt a State heartily. Here is an extract from the NET that signifies the fact. The question arises

Why don't Sikhs rise up against India and join Pakistan? The answer is given by a Sikh, which is high- lighted here.

I am a Sikh. A few days ago, my brother asked my father,"Papa, some Sikhs wanted Khalistan. Would it be beneficial for all the sikhs?"

My dad said,"Nothing would have changed if Khalistan was made except currency and government. And, the government is the same everywhere. **We are happy being a part of India**".

So here the point is - being Sikhs, anybody or any Sikh family is happy being a part of India. Every Sikh doesn't want Khalistan. Haters are everywhere. Yes, some people do have some complaints about the government, but everywhere Indians are not alone. Everyone has complaints. Every government has loopholes. Proper solution by negotiation is the answer, if not rule of administration as done by Modi in Gujarat unlike GANDHI is the answer but no matter people might have designed it "Gujarat Riot is nothing but Modi Riot ". People throughout the World once discarded Modi but now everywhere Modi is for World Peace.

Formation of a different country is not the solution. If so then, every single religion will ask for a new country. It's not the solution but it is the problem. We are not against any religion and this is the truth. Most of the Sikhs are happy being a part of India.

THE END